JUN 1 3 2016

KEEP
~ it ~
# VEGAN

KEEP ~it~ VEGAN

OVER
100
SIMPLE, HEALTHY
& DELICIOUS DISHES

Áine Carlin

PHOTOGRAPHY BY ALI ALLEN

KYLE BOOKS

TO MY MOM AND DAD FOR ALWAYS SUPPORTING ME.
MY SISTER MAIRÉAD FOR ALWAYS BELIEVING IN ME
AND MY DARLING HUSBAND JASON FOR ALWAYS LOVING ME.

Published in 2015 by Kyle Books
www.kylebooks.com
general.enquiries@kylebooks.com

Distributed by National Book Network
4501 Forbes Blvd., Suite 200
Lanham, MD 20706
Phone: (800) 462-6420
Fax: (800) 338-4550
customercare@nbnbooks.com

First published in Great Britain in 2014 by
Kyle Books, an imprint of Kyle Cathie Ltd.

10 9 8 7 6 5 4 3 2 1

ISBN 978-1-909487-21-5

Project Editor: Tara O'Sullivan
Copy Editor: Jane Bamforth
Proofreader: Ruth Baldwin
Designer: Nicky Collings
Photographer: Ali Allen
Illustrator: Aaron Blecha
Food Stylist: Linda Tubby
Production: Nic Jones and Gemma John

Library of Congress Control
Number: 2014947995

Color reproduction by ALTA London
Printed and bound in China by C&C
Offset Printing Co., Ltd.

CONTENTS

INTRODUCTION

Welcome to *Keep it Vegan*, my first ever plant-based recipe book, which I really hope will speak to everyone with a love of food and, more importantly… eating! Whether it be the novice vegan currently finding their way, experienced vegan cooks seeking a few more simple dishes to add to their already existing menu arsenal, or even the curious omnivore, who quite frankly wants to know what all the fuss is about—everybody is welcome at my table. Take as little or as much as you want from the book and feel free to experiment with the recipes themselves… in my opinion there is no one way, and everybody's palate is different and valid. For some the dishes will be an introduction to a whole new way of cooking, and for others it might just be a twist on a vegan classic that they are already familiar with, but rest assured each and every one of them comes directly from my heart and kitchen, and will hopefully find a new home in your happy space, too.

Before we get way ahead of ourselves, though, let me begin by explaining the purpose of this book and what makes it so special to me. Not that long ago (I'll be celebrating my fourth veganiversary this year!) I was a habitual meat-eater and, more significantly for me, a devout dairy consumer to boot… ice cream, cheese, yogurt—you name it I ate it, and with gusto at that. Although I was always anti-fast food, it never even crossed my mind to question where my food came from.

Until, that is, I embarked on the learning journey that has led me to where I am today. Along the way, I found a new respect for my body, became much healthier, and even discovered a whole new level of love for cooking. All in all, it may have been one of the best decisions I've ever made. Now, I'm not here to convert you to veganism. What I'm interested in is opening your eyes to the world of possibilities that lie before you when you take meat and dairy out of the equation and focus on all the wondrous ingredients normally relegated to the "side dish" by showing you how to make them take center stage.

This then is a book about food. Plain and simple. Without being over-fussy or complicated I hope to share just a few of my favorite recipes that I use frequently in my own kitchen and along the way help you to see that a life without animal products really ain't so bad. In fact, it's kinda wonderful.

FROM MEAT-EATER TO VEGAN

You may be wondering how a full-blown omnivore suddenly went vegan overnight… and it was quite literally overnight. To be honest, it came as a surprise even to me, as I'd never even entertained the idea of becoming vegetarian, let alone immersing myself in a lifestyle that I'd believed to be restrictive and boring. I was (and still am) a total foodie, the kind of person whose thoughts turn to dinner immediately after finishing lunch.

When my husband and I moved to Chicago for two years, I was in foodie heaven. I spent hours scouring the supermarket, cheering at the reasonable prices—especially when it came to the meat and dairy products. Not only were we eating well (or so we thought), our budget was healthier than ever. But about a year into our new lifestyle, you could say we were starting to feel the burn. Even though we had convinced ourselves we were eating a healthy, balanced diet, our bodies were starting to tell a very different story. We were both feeling lethargic, had gained a little weight and physically felt the worst we had in years—and we were only in our 20s. It soon became clear the source of the problem was food.

At the time there was a lot of discussion about high fructose corn syrup (HFCS), a hideous laboratory-born sweetener that should be avoided at all costs. However, I soon discovered it was in everything, and I do mean everything… bread, cookies, drinks, and a whole host of other foods that you would never dream contain such a thing. Aha, I thought! This is it. And so I started cleaning up our diet. Even though I rarely bought typical processed foods, this was still a difficult task, given the fact that HFCS manages to find its way into the least likely products. But once you're on that path, it can be hard to turn back and so I began to look into farm practices and specifically the meat we had been consuming daily—and to say I was horrified would be an understatement.

My only option was to remove myself from the situation and forge a new way for myself and my husband (who was on board from the beginning). Ultimately that decision led me to veganism. It really was a case of going to bed an omnivore and waking up vegan—once I'd equipped myself with the relevant info, there was no looking back. While I'm sure my friends and family didn't fully "get it" to begin with, but they have since become my biggest supporters. You will always encounter people who question your lifestyle choices, and they won't always be pleasant or simply "curious." Vegans are often accused of being angry or consumed with an overriding animal-rights agenda, so I feel it's my duty to show a different side to a lifestyle that can be off-putting to many. Positive actions are the order of the day; keep your cool and you'll find it much easier to keep it vegan.

Although my health led me to consider veganism, let me be clear it was ultimately the plight of the animals that made my mind up—it was that simple. The most important thing to me was reducing any further suffering by my own hands. Veganism gave me the confidence to become the person I always thought I could be… compassionate, caring, and open-hearted, and it also gave me the strength of my convictions to do other things that were nothing to do with my diet—writing being just one of them. And because I feel it gave me the voice I knew I'd been lacking all these years, I realized the perfect way to return the favor was to write this book and help others discover the many virtues of veganism.

It's not about lending another "holier than thou" attitude to the mix. I'd much rather make you smile with a slice of chocolate cake or fill your belly with a wholesome stew. The truth is in the eating, and there couldn't be a more relevant saying when it comes to eating vegan. And remember, if a meat and potatoes Irish chick can do it, anybody can.

HEALTH AND BODY BENEFITS

OK, OK, so you've given us the spiel, now give us the details, I hear you cry! So, here goes. The health benefits that stem from leading a vegan diet are impressive. I can only give you solid information on what we have experienced first-hand, yet you don't have to look very far to find similar stories and examples of how veganism has improved people's lives. I know my husband won't mind me saying this (and too bad if he does, ha!), but prior to adopting a vegan diet we both may have had a teeny… hmmm, now how should I put this?… perspiration problem. Maybe it was down to what they like to call "the meat sweats"; however, let me just say we went through a lot of deodorant and wearing a t-shirt two days in a row wasn't even an option. Now that problem is a thing of the past. I know it seems crazy, yet it's totally true. Of course, we still sweat, it's only natural, but the odor is different and our pits are so dry, wearing the same tee all week long would not be an issue—not that I would ever do that. Ahem.

The next thing we noticed was our quality of sleep. At the time we cut out animal products, we were two lethargic messes—I could barely get out of bed in the morning. It took several weeks for our bodies to adjust, but if I were to estimate a timeframe, I certainly noticed a difference at the three-week mark. Not only were we sleeping more soundly but we were waking up refreshed—for once in my life, I actually felt rested, whereas before I could've slept for 12 hours straight and still struggle to get up.

Same goes for my energy levels. After the initial detox period, when your body is ridding itself of all those toxins delivered straight into your bloodstream thanks to meat and dairy, you will notice a strangely stimulating, continuous buzz, and that "buzz" is energy. The urge to get up and do things (even if it's just tidying the kitchen or changing my bed linen) is so great that my fitness levels have vastly improved as a result of these small but consistent bursts of activity.

With a propensity for over-thinking things and even experiencing quite dark periods, I can safely say that veganism has helped my outlook and general mental health. That's not to say I still don't have my meltdowns or fragile moments, but I can cope better, with a clearer mind, and I feel less despairing when they happen.

Skin, hair, and nails are surely the main things that are a sign of good health. Before I went vegan, I was prone to greasy skin, had dry, brittle hair that certainly did not shine, my nails were always fragile, and hangnails were the bane of my life. I'm not saying it was an *et voilà* makeover transformation, but there is a marked improvement in all of these areas of my physical appearance. Specifically, my hair now has a natural, healthy shine, which many people comment on (no, it's not dyed!), my skin is clear with rarely any unwanted t-zone shine, plus my nails are bullet-strong with not a hangnail in sight. Because I feel so in-tune with my body now, I can see a difference when I'm not hydrated enough, have been eating too much sugar, or been slacking on my whole foods—it's a wonderful thing once you realize you can control and improve your appearance just by altering something in your lifestyle.

People often ask, "Does going vegan help you lose weight?" and I would hesitantly say, "Yes." Why the hesitancy? Because it's entirely dependent on what you

choose to eat—sugar, alcohol, and oils are all vegan, but they definitely won't make you skinny. There are many vegans who never experience any weight loss (and that's not to say they aren't healthy—everyone's body works in different ways), but in my case I would have to say it's been the only time in my life where my weight has been stable. I've never exactly struggled with my weight and for the most part have erred on the side of slim, yet it's certainly fluctuated throughout the years and I was definitely not my ideal weight at my wedding, much to my dismay. My problem areas have always been my bottom, thighs, and legs and I tend to carry all my excess weight in these places. However, I noticed a colossal change in shape several months into my new vegan lifestyle, which gave me the courage to be braver with my fashion choices. I'll never be rail-thin but now, in my 30s, I can safely say I am more content with my body than I ever have been and it is all thanks to veganism and the plant-based foods I am currently eating.

Any regrets?

Flip back to the start and read through the sentence where I told you how much I loved dairy. LOVED. IT. So much so, I can honestly say I feel like I had a full-blown relationship with it—which would make you think the breaking-up process may have been a difficult one, right? I really wish there was a struggle-and-strife story I could feed you, one where I expose the grieving I did for ice cream or the mourning period when I pushed cheese out of my life forever, but the answer is no. I don't have any story other than the one where I embraced a new lifestyle that still includes deliciously authentic ice cream, wonderful plant-based cheeses, and a magnificent array of yogurts that satisfy every urge, need, or craving. You see, we're lucky. We live in the age of veganism, where every product you can think of has a vegan equivalent. The ingredients are all there waiting for you if you need them—they might not be ingredients I reach for or rely on frequently,

but occasionally the urge takes over and you know you need them. My weakness was always Greek yogurt in the morning; however, now that I've discovered the coconut equivalent, it's a distant memory. Same goes for ice cream… there are so many varieties on the market now, you can often be spoiled for choice. Nut-based, soy-based, coconut-based—whatever your requirements, you will be able to find a solution. It's so easy to keep it vegan that I rarely consciously think of myself as "a vegan"—I'm just someone who likes to eat!

Go forth and conquer!

Whether you're dabbling in veganism or fully committed, there are many ways to enjoy this magnificent lifestyle and cuisine. Maybe it will open you up to a range of ingredients that you've yet to explore or allow you to experiment with existing flavors that continue to excite you. What matters is that you have fun, keep an open mind, and create some delicious food… regardless of the intent or outcome. Leave the pressure at the door and go into the kitchen with a view to conquering any vegan-induced fears through cooking—and, really, is there any better way?

PANTRY ESSENTIALS

Because I tend to do smaller store trips for my perishables, I like to have a pantry stocked full of cans and jars that can turn a simple selection of vegetables into a delicious evening meal in no time. From Dijon mustard to yeast extract, they all play a pivotal role in my cooking and can often transform a dish from fine to fantastic. I'm not afraid to use a pinch of sugar here and there, and I'm all about the saying "If it ain't broke, don't fix it," which is why you'll see many of these ingredients used time and again in my recipes—also crucial when you're on a budget like myself.

In my vegan cupboard
I tend to avoid things like egg-replacer and arrowroot because I feel if I can get away with using a banana and some baking soda, then I will. Make life simple, that's my motto. *And* as you'll soon see, my style is all about stripping things back to the bare minimum without compromising on flavor... so it's time to get that barren pantry prepped—let's do this!

Beans, pulses, legumes, dried fruit, nuts, and grains
Beans and pulses (a selection including chickpeas, black beans, kidney beans)
Brown basmati rice
Bulgur wheat
Couscous
Dried legumes (red lentils, split peas, etc.)
Oats
Pasta
Polenta
Quinoa
Selection of nuts and dried fruit

Coconut products
Coconut cream
Coconut milk
Shredded coconut

Flours and baking products
Baking powder
Baking soda
Cornstarch
Flour (all-purpose, whole-wheat, and chickpea)

Oils
Coconut oil
Extra virgin olive oil
Olive oil
Sesame oil
Sunflower or peanut oil

Savory sauces, seasonings, and flavorings
Balsamic vinegar
Capers
Cider vinegar
Dijon mustard
Peppercorns
Red wine vinegar
Sea salt
Sushi vinegar
Sweet chili sauce
Tamari or soy sauce
Vegetable bouillon cubes
Whole-grain mustard
Yeast extract

Sugars and sweet flavorings
Sugar (several types, including confectioners' sugar)
Agave nectar
Maple syrup
Orange blossom water
Rose water
Vanilla extract

Tomato products
Canned tomatoes
Tomato paste
Tomato sauce

In my vegan fridge

I have a handful of refrigerated goods that I use fairly infrequently, but it's good to have a few on rotation for those times when you're in the mood for cake or wanting to whip up an über-quick dip. I sporadically utilize these ingredients throughout the book. However, I by no means recommend relying on them—treat them as a fun "now-and-again" alternative to those foods you might occasionally be missing.

Dairy-free mayo
Hummus
Plant milks (soy, almond, coconut)
Soy cream
Soy yogurt
Tofu (marinated and firm)
Vegan margarine
Vegan wine—not all wines are created equal! Some undergo a fining process that involves the use of animal products. Luckily most major supermarkets make life easy for us by slapping on a label that says explicitly which wines are vegan and which aren't, and you can usually find the information you need on "vegan wine sites" all over the web. Cheers!

In my vegan freezer

My freezer is probably the least stocked of all my food storage areas, but that's not to say it doesn't hold some vital components—after all, who can really live a fulfilled life without (dairy-free) ice cream? The frozen veggies are crucial for curries, dips, stews, and more, and while the selection varies from time to time, I always make sure to have peas and fava beans… there is a multitude of dishes that can be saved with some green-pea action. When my bananas fully ripen, I try to keep at least two (peeled and chopped) in the freezer for smoothies and instant soft serve— you'll not believe how reliant you'll become on them.

Fava beans
Peas
Sweet corn
Vanilla vegan ice cream

Fresh herbs

With regards to fresh herbs, it might be wise to let you know now that I like to think of them in degrees of relationship (strange—*moi*?)… that is, how close or not I am to each one. For example, you should consider flat-leaf parsley, cilantro, and basil your closest friends; thyme, rosemary, and mint your buddies; tarragon and dill very good acquaintances. Use them this way, and your food will be a whole lot better for it.

Dried herbs

Some herbs cannot be substituted so easily for the dried variety, which is why I encourage you to stick to the following lest you end up with some very funky flavors.

Bay leaves
Herbs de Provence
Oregano
Thyme

Spices

Where would we be without a little spice in our lives? I've come to fall in love with cumin, have a long-held affection for smoked paprika, and am forever lusting after nutmeg… there I go with the relationship thing again!

Cardamom pods
Cayenne pepper
Chile flakes
Chinese five-spice powder
Cinnamon sticks
Cloves
Cumin
Garam masala
Ground allspice
Ground cardamom
Ground cinnamon
Ground nutmeg
Mild curry powder
Nutmeg
Smoked paprika
Star anise
Turmeric

I could probably add to this list all day, but if you have at least some of these essentials in your pantry, you've already won half the battle.

Breakfast, BRUNCH & MORE

BIRCHER MUESLI

COCOA AND ALMOND BUTTER
OVERNIGHT OATS

SNICKERDOODLE QUINOA BOWL
WITH APPLE SLICES

BREAKFAST BROWNIE WITH A
STRAWBERRY BOTTOM

COCONUT, DATE, AND ALMOND
GRANOLA

BANANA AND MANGO FROZEN
DESSERT

SUMMER BERRY "BUTTERMILK"
PANCAKES

ROSEMARY-AND-PEAR-STUFFED
FRENCH TOAST

CHEWY NUTTY BREAKFAST BREAD

MORNING OATJACKS

GLUTEN-FREE BLUEBERRY MUFFINS

TOASTED BREAKFAST BURRITO

BAKED BRUNCHTIME MUSHROOMS

SIMPLE SCRAMBLED TOFU

SAVORY PUDLA PANCAKE

VEGETABLE ROSTI WITH A SMOKY
ROASTED SALSA

SUPER GREEN SMOOTHIE

bircher MUESLI

serves 2

This early-20th-century favorite is still a mainstay for many at breakfast time. Developed by Maximilian Bircher-Brenner at the beginning of the 1900s, its condensed-milk-containing origins have been given a slightly healthier spin over the years, so consider this non-dairy vegan version another nutritional progression. Grated apple and soy yogurt make this a substantial, sweet, and seriously satisfying start to the day, and one I rely on more often than I care to admit.

INGREDIENTS

1¾ cups rolled oats
½ cup rice milk (or other plant milk)
1 apple
1 tablespoon raisins or golden raisins
1 tablespoon chopped hazelnuts
¼ cup plain soy yogurt
1 teaspoon agave nectar
1 tablespoon mixed seeds
1 tablespoon shredded coconut

METHOD

1 Place the oats in a bowl and pour in the rice milk. Cover with a lid and refrigerate overnight.

2 In the morning, grate the apple and add to the soaked oats along with the raisins, nuts, yogurt, and agave nectar. Stir to combine and top with the mixed seeds and coconut.

Variations

You could also add fresh berries or dust with a little ground cinnamon or hemp powder.

cocoa and almond butter
OVERNIGHT OATS

serves 1

I'm all about breakfast. Oats, polenta, pancakes, granola, bread. You name it, I make it. I love mixing it up in the mornings and while I do have my favorites I also have a pretty short attention span when it comes to recipes. I have an insatiable need to improve upon them, and what better time to do this than first thing in the morning? I find it sets me up for the day and inspires my cooking and eating choices thereafter.

And if you thought overnight oats were over you'd be so totally wrong. They are endlessly versatile and I never tire of thinking up various combos for mine. This version might seem a little bit indulgent for some but it's full of good stuff, too, so there's no need to feel bad after a bowlful.

Because this recipe uses unsweetened cocoa powder, you get that lovely chocolate flavor *sans* the sugar and the dried cranberries add enough sweetness and chew anyway—a great alternative to chocolate-coated cereal for kids and always popular with grown-ups, too!

INGREDIENTS

3 tablespoons rolled oats

1 teaspoon unsweetened cocoa powder

¼ cup oat milk (or other plant milk)

3 tablespoons chopped almonds

3 tablespoons dried cranberries

1 tablespoon shredded coconut

1 heaping teaspoon almond butter

agave nectar, for drizzling (optional)

METHOD

1 Place the oats and cocoa powder in a bowl and thoroughly mix. Pour in the oat milk, adding a little more if it looks too dry, cover, and leave in the fridge overnight to soak.

2 In the morning give the oats a good stir and top with the almonds and cranberries. Sprinkle the coconut over the oats and dollop the almond butter in the center. If you are using the agave nectar, lightly drizzle it all over.

SNICKERDOODLE
QUINOA BOWL
with apple slices
serves 4

Not just a lunch or dinnertime option, the almighty Andean quinoa (pronounced "keen-wah") grain is also an excellent breakfast alternative that is packed full of protein and incredibly filling too. If you're bored with oats but still hanker after a warming bowl of cereal in the morning, this cinnamon-infused milky bowl of greatness might just be for you. The addictive caramelized apple slices only add to this year-round recipe that is sure to bring a smile to even the groggiest of morning people. And if you don't want to make it from scratch first thing (it happens), simply whip it up the night before and gently warm it through on the stove with an additional splash of milk the next day. Granted the word "snickerdoodle" might normally conjure up images of sugar cookies, but this deliciously spiced breakfast bowl more than lives up to its cinnamony name, giving its German pastry past a serious run for its money.

INGREDIENTS

For the quinoa
1½ cups almond milk, plus extra
to serve
¼ cup agave nectar
1 teaspoon ground cinnamon
¼ teaspoon freshly grated nutmeg
1 cinnamon stick
2 cardamom pods
1 cup quinoa

For the caramelized apples
2 Granny Smith apples, peeled,
cored, and sliced
1 teaspoon ground cinnamon
3 tablespoons maple syrup

METHOD

1 In a medium-sized bowl, whisk together the almond milk, agave nectar, ground cinnamon, and nutmeg. Pour the mixture into a medium-sized pan. Add the cinnamon stick and cardamom pods and bring the milk mixture to a gentle boil. Pour in the quinoa, reduce the heat to a simmer, and cover. Stir frequently to prevent burning and, once the liquid has been absorbed (after about 20 minutes), take off the heat. Remove the cinnamon stick and cardamom pods.

2 Place the apples in a frying pan along with the ground cinnamon and maple syrup. Bring to a gentle simmer and cook until the apples are soft and sticky, about 15 minutes.

3 Serve the quinoa in small bowls with a splash of almond milk and topped with the caramelized apple slices.

BREAKFAST BROWNIE
with a strawberry bottom

serves 2

Truth be told, prior to my vegan conversion, chocolate was never much on my radar—sickly sweet milk chocolate bars were just never really my thing. Since embracing a world without dairy, however, I find that my appreciation for that most luxurious of confectionary treats has blossomed into a full-on obsession, which is why I had to devise a way of making it a valid breakfast option. Striking that elusive balance between indulgence and virtue isn't always easy, but with strawberries, cocoa, and dark chocolate chips in the mix, oatmeal need never be dull again. Not exactly your traditional bowl of oatmeal, this baked variety is dense and rich, with a texture that alludes to everyone's all-time favorite dessert... the humble but yummy brownie. The bonus here, though, is that you get to have it "before"—hurray!

INGREDIENTS

¾ cup almond milk
1 heaping tablespoon unsweetened
cocoa powder
1 tablespoon agave nectar or
maple syrup
1 teaspoon vanilla extract
pinch of coarse salt
3½ cups rolled oats
2 tablespoons chocolate chips
1 cup strawberries, hulled and
halved

METHOD

1 Preheat the oven to 350°F.

2 In a medium bowl, whisk the almond milk, cocoa powder, agave nectar or syrup, and vanilla extract together until combined.

3 Add a pinch of salt to the oats before mixing with the wet ingredients. Stir in the chocolate chips.

4 Divide the strawberries equally between two heatproof bowls. Pour in the oat mixture and bake in the oven for 15 to 20 minutes.

5 Remove from the oven and eat warm.

TIP
Top with a little more almond milk or agave nectar for extra yumminess

coconut, date, and
ALMOND GRANOLA

serves 8 to 10

Granola is a staple at our breakfast table. So much so, I began to realize I was forking out a fortune for the stuff, which led me to creating this simple recipe that is easier on the pocket and even better on the palate. You can mix and match whichever nuts and dried fruit you prefer, but I adore this coconut, date, and almond combo because it's so sweetly satisfying without feeling over-virtuous. Pair with fresh fruit and thick coconut yogurt for a seriously indulgent start to your morning.

INGREDIENTS

1 teaspoon sunflower or
coconut oil
½ cup maple syrup
1 teaspoon vanilla extract
2¾ cups rolled oats
½ teaspoon ground cinnamon
¾ cup whole almonds
¾ cup pumpkin seeds
½ cup shredded coconut
½ cup sliced almonds
½ cup pitted dried dates, chopped
fresh fruit and coconut yogurt,
to serve

METHOD

1 Preheat the oven to 300°F.

2 Whisk the oil, syrup, and vanilla extract together in a small bowl.

3 Place the oats on a baking sheet, sprinkle with the cinnamon, and stir to coat before lightly toasting in the oven for 10 minutes.

4 Next, add the whole almonds, pumpkin seeds, and half the shredded coconut and stir to combine. Pour the syrup mixture over the granola, stir well to coat completely, and bake for another 15 minutes. Add the sliced almonds and bake for a final 5 to 10 minutes.

5 Remove from the oven, add the remaining coconut and the chopped dates, and stir well. Set aside to cool completely before transferring to an airtight lidded container, where it will keep for up to two weeks.

6 Serve with fresh fruit and coconut yogurt.

banana and mango
FROZEN DESSERT

serves 1 to 2

Something magical happens to frozen fruit when it's blended. For me it's as good as eating ice cream, and this fruit combo is my absolute favorite. Halfway between a smoothie and soft-serve ice cream, it's better scooped up by the spoonful but, by all means, if you want to use a straw, be my guest.

INGREDIENTS

1 banana
1 mango
½ cup coconut milk
handful of frozen berries, to serve
(optional)

METHOD

1 Peel the banana and peel and pit the mango. Slice both into medium-sized pieces. Place the fruit in a freezer bag and seal, or in an airtight lidded container, and freeze overnight.

2 The next day, put the frozen banana and mango and the coconut milk into a blender and blend until completely smooth. Serve immediately in a glass—I sometimes serve this in a mason jar, decorated with a selection of frozen berries.

SUMMER BERRY
"buttermilk"
PANCAKES

makes 8 to 10 pancakes / serves 2 to 4

Pancakes are perfect brunch time fodder and a sure-fire way to get your weekend off to a good start as well as impressing guests. This basic mixture can be tweaked and added to as desired (blueberries, chocolate chips, or raisins work wonderfully too), but I just love this candied walnut and nutmeg combo.

INGREDIENTS

For the pancakes
1¼ cups all-purpose flour
¼ cup superfine sugar
1½ teaspoons baking powder
1 teaspoon baking soda
pinch of sea salt
½ teaspoon freshly grated nutmeg
1 cup soy milk
1 teaspoon cider vinegar
1 banana, peeled and mashed
1 tablespoon soy butter
1 tablespoon sunflower oil plus
extra for cooking

For the candied walnuts
¾ cup walnut pieces
1 tablespoon agave nectar

To serve
fresh berries
freshly grated nutmeg
agave nectar or maple syrup

METHOD

1 In a large bowl, thoroughly combine the dry pancake ingredients. Mix together the soy milk and cider vinegar in a bowl, set aside for several minutes, and allow to curdle—this will be the "buttermilk" element.

2 Whisk the banana into the soy milk mixture. Make a well in the dry ingredients and add the milk mixture, folding gently until incorporated.

3 Melt the butter with the oil in a medium, non-stick frying pan and pour into the bowl, ensuring everything is fully incorporated—I use a whisk. Let the pancake mix sit for a while—the pancakes will puff up better.

4 Preheat the oven to 250°F. Heat a little more oil in the frying pan and add a small ladleful of mixture to form a pancake. Don't overcrowd the pan—only cook one or two pancakes at a time. They should come to about 3in in diameter. Cook until bubbles appear on the surface before flipping over and cooking for another few minutes on the other side. Transfer to a plate and keep the pancakes warm in the oven—try not to stack them or they may get soggy.

5 Wipe the pan with paper towels, add the walnuts, and toast over medium heat for a few minutes before adding the agave. Allow the walnuts to become sticky and then slightly hard—stir constantly so they don't stick to the pan.

6 Serve the pancakes with fresh berries, the candied walnuts, a good grating of nutmeg, and drizzles of agave or maple syrup. Brunch time!

rosemary-and-pear-stuffed
FRENCH TOAST

serves 2

Rosemary might not be the most obvious choice here, but trust me when I tell you that it will infuse the pears with a delicate herby flavor that is both fragrant and delicious. You could say I have a thing for unusual combinations—admittedly with sometimes less than impressive results, ahem. Thankfully, though, this recipe was a success story, with the rosemary lending an essential layer to an otherwise simple dish.

INGREDIENTS

For the whipped coconut cream
1 × 14oz can coconut milk,
chilled overnight
3/4 cup confectioners' sugar
1 teaspoon vanilla extract

For the pears
2 pears, peeled, cored and sliced
1/4 cup maple syrup
1 sprig rosemary

For the toast
1 banana, peeled
1 3/4 cups coconut milk drink
(from a carton, not canned milk)
1 teaspoon vanilla extract
1 tablespoon cornstarch
1/4 teaspoon ground cinnamon
pinch of freshly grated nutmeg
1 tablespoon agave nectar
4 thick slices crusty white bread
2 tablespoons sunflower oil
1 tablespoon vegan margarine

METHOD

1 Remove the can of coconut milk from the fridge and carefully spoon off the now-hardened top layer into a mixing bowl—once you hit the liquid layer, stop. Add the sugar and vanilla extract and whisk vigorously with an electric mixer until fluffy and smooth. Put in the fridge until required.

2 Place the pear slices in a medium, non-stick frying pan along with the maple syrup and whole rosemary sprig and bring to a very gentle simmer. Cook for around 5 minutes or until the pears just begin to soften before carefully turning them over to cook for another 4 to 5 minutes on the other side. Remove the rosemary sprig and transfer the pears to a dish until needed. Wipe the pan with paper towels.

3 In a large, shallow dish, mash the banana and then whisk or blend it together with the coconut milk drink, vanilla extract, cornstarch, cinnamon, nutmeg, and agave until smooth. Arrange the pears and bread in two sandwiches.

4 Place the pear sandwiches into the banana and coconut mixture and let them absorb the liquid for 10 minutes, turning halfway through.

5 Heat the oil and margarine together in the frying pan over medium heat. Add the sandwiches. Press firmly with the back of a spatula to compress the bread and ensure it gets golden on the bottom. Cook the sandwiches for 5 to 7 minutes on each side. Remove from the pan and serve hot with a spoonful of the whipped coconut cream.

chewy nutty BREAKFAST BREAD

makes 1 × 1lb loaf

Toast can certainly get boring in the mornings, yet that still doesn't negate my craving for bread first thing. The list of ingredients may appear a little long (and it is) but just one of these loaves should last you a good few days—or feed a large group as a healthy(ish) brunch option. While white flour is not always my first choice, I often find that a loaf containing 100 percent whole wheat can be a tricky one to master and is pretty dense in texture. The combination of flours and flaxseed here renders the bread chewy, nutty, and deeply satisfying… I might not recommend it every day, but once in a while it's a wonderful breakfast treat.

INGREDIENTS

soy butter, for greasing
1 1/2 cups all-purpose flour
2/3 cup whole wheat flour
1/3 cup rolled oats
3 tablespoons ground flaxseed
1 teaspoon baking powder
1/2 teaspoon baking soda
1 banana, peeled
3/4 cup soy milk (or other plant milk, such as coconut milk)
1/4 cup soy yogurt
1 teaspoon cider vinegar
1/4 cup sunflower oil
1/2 cup agave nectar (or other vegan sweetener)
1/4 cup pitted prunes, roughly chopped
1/2 cup walnuts, roughly chopped

METHOD

1 Preheat the oven to 350°F. Grease a 1lb loaf pan.

2 Place the flours, oats, and ground flaxseed in a large mixing bowl. Add to the bowl along with the baking powder and baking soda and stir well to combine.

3 Purée or mash the banana and whisk together with the soy milk, soy yogurt, cider vinegar, oil, and agave until thoroughly combined.

4 Make a well in the center of the dry ingredients and pour in the wet mixture and banana purée. Fold gently to combine everything thoroughly. Fold the prunes and walnuts through the mixture before transferring it to the greased loaf pan. Level the surface with the back of a spoon. You might also want to give the pan a firm tap on the work surface to remove any air bubbles.

5 Bake in the oven for about 1 hour or until an inserted skewer comes out clean. Let the loaf cool in the pan, then transfer to a wire cooling rack to cool completely before slicing. Store in an airtight container—if you're not eating it all right away! This is delicious sliced and spread with vegan butter.

morning OATJACKS

serves 8 to 10

Sometimes mornings are all about the grab 'n' go scenario. It's all very well having recipes that you can prepare and eat at your leisure, but realistically this rarely ever happens, which is exactly where these oatjacks come into play. Now, I'm not saying they are wholly virtuous (hello, sweetener and margerine!), but there's enough goodness packed into these little squares to tide you over until lunchtime, when you'll be making up for it with a bowl of rice and kale. Right?

INGREDIENTS

soy butter, for greasing
1¾ cups steel-cut oats
⅓ cup raisins
4 medjool dates, pitted and chopped
½ cup walnuts or pecans, chopped
½ cup mixed seeds
¼ cup shredded coconut
3 tablespoons vegan margarine
½ cup agave nectar
½ cup maple syrup

METHOD

1 Preheat the oven to 350°F. Grease a 9in baking sheet and line it with parchment paper.

2 In a large bowl combine the oats, raisins, dates, nuts, seeds, and coconut. Stir well to combine.

3 Place the margarine, agave, and maple syrup in a small saucepan and heat gently until the mixture begins to bubble, then remove from the heat.

4 Pour the melted mixture over the oat mixture and stir to incorporate, ensuring everything is coated with the syrup.

5 Transfer to the lined baking sheet and pack the mixture in tightly, pressing it down with the back of a spatula.

6 Bake in the oven for 30 minutes, then remove and, while still in the pan, gently mark out squares using a knife (do not cut the whole way through at this stage). Once the cooked mixture is completely cool, cut it into squares. Keep in an airtight container for up to 1 week.

GLUTEN-FREE *blueberry* MUFFINS

makes 6 large muffins

Nothing beats a cup of joe and a freshly baked blueberry muffin in the morning… even better if it happens to be gluten-free and *sans* refined sugar and oil. I refuse to forfeit the sweetness altogether (hence the maple syrup and colossal amount of berries) and, in fact, this muffin recipe really benefits from as many of those berry blues as possible, so feel free to pop a few extra on top before baking. Best eaten the day after baking (if you can wait that long!)—it allows the wonderfully ink-like blueberry juice to really penetrate the muffin, making them a great option to cook in advance. Although I don't personally avoid gluten, I prefer the texture and taste of the chickpea flour used here. The only drawback is trying to limit myself to one!

INGREDIENTS

1 cup gram (chickpea) flour
$^{1}/_{2}$ cup ground almonds
$^{1}/_{4}$ cup shredded coconut
$^{1}/_{2}$ teaspoon baking soda
$^{3}/_{4}$ teaspoon baking powder
1 banana, peeled and mashed,
or 3 tablespoons apple purée
$^{1}/_{2}$ cup almond milk
1 teaspoon vanilla extract
$^{1}/_{3}$ cup maple syrup
1$^{1}/_{2}$ cups blueberries

METHOD

1 Preheat the oven to 350°F. Line a muffin pan with 6 muffin liners.

2 Lightly mix the flour, ground almonds, coconut, baking soda, and baking powder together until combined.

3 Place the mashed banana or apple purée in a bowl. Whisk the almond milk, vanilla extract, and syrup into the fruit.

4 Make a well in the center of the flour mixture and pour in the almond milk mix. Fold gently until combined—be careful not to overwork the batter.

5 Finally, fold through the blueberries and carefully spoon into the muffin liners, filling them to just under $^{1}/_{2}$in from the top. Bake in the oven for 20 to 25 minutes. Set aside to cool on a wire cooling rack. These will keep in an airtight container for several days.

toasted BREAKFAST BURRITO

serves 4

This requires a little longer in the kitchen than is normally viable for weekdays, so I like to keep it as a weekend brunch option… but, boy, is it worth the wait. The scramble and bean combo is a double dose of protein that will set you up really well for the rest of the day.

INGREDIENTS

For the beans
1 tablespoon olive oil
1 onion, finely chopped
salt and black pepper
1 × 14oz can pinto or borlotti beans
1 teaspoon ground cumin
½ teaspoon smoked paprika
1 vegetable bouillon cube
1 teaspoon tomato paste
1 tablespoon finely chopped
flat-leaf parsley

For the guacamole
1 avocado
juice of 1 lime
¾ cup fresh cilantro

For the tofu
1 tablespoon olive oil
1 scallion, chopped
7oz firm tofu, drained and pressed
(see page 33)
1 teaspoon garlic powder

METHOD

1 For the beans, heat the oil in a heavy-bottomed saucepan, add the onion, season, and sweat until soft. Drain and rinse the beans and add them to the pan along with the cumin and paprika, and stir to coat. Cook for a few minutes before crumbling in the vegetable bouillon cube. Stir in the tomato paste and ½ cup cold water. Thoroughly mix and bring to a gentle simmer for 10 to 15 minutes or until the water has been absorbed, stirring occasionally. When it's ready, stir in the parsley.

2 To make the guacamole, roughly chop the avocado into cubes, season with salt, pour in the lime juice, and stir in the cilantro. Set aside.

3 Next, make the scrambled tofu. Heat the oil in a medium, non-stick frying pan. Cook the scallions for a few seconds before crumbling in the tofu. Sprinkle in the garlic powder, turmeric, and sea salt. Stir to combine until the turmeric is completely dispersed. Whisk together the mustard and vinegar, pour in the tofu, and cook the mixture for 10 to 15 minutes, stirring occasionally. Taste for seasoning before transferring the scramble to a bowl. Wash and dry the frying pan and return it to the heat.

4 Lay the tortillas on a work surface. Divide the spinach between each one, placing it in the middle section, followed by the beans, scramble, and guacamole. Add a generous splash of Tabasco before folding. Fold both the shorter ends in first. Holding the center with a thumb, fold down the other two sides. Carefully turn each tortilla over and place onto the hot, dry frying

INGREDIENTS

½ teaspoon ground turmeric
½ teaspoon sea salt
¼ teaspoon Dijon mustard
¼ teaspoon cider vinegar

4 large whole wheat flour tortillas
3 cups baby spinach
Tabasco sauce, to taste

METHOD

pan—you should be able to fit in two at a time. Allow the tortillas to toast for 4 to 5 minutes, then turn them over using tongs and cook them for a similar length of time on the other side.

5 Lift the tortillas onto a cutting board, using the tongs, and cut diagonally using a sharp knife before serving.

baked brunchtime MUSHROOMS

serves 4

I make these yummy mushrooms far more frequently than is probably normal. The coconut milk is a rich addition but if seasoned correctly doesn't stand out as a distinct flavor and merely lends an unctuous creaminess to the spinach and leek mixture. You could easily add another element on top (nutritional yeast or bread crumbs work well) but they bake so beautifully in the oven it almost seems a shame to mess with their already existing perfection.

INGREDIENTS

4 portobello mushrooms
1 tablespoon extra virgin olive oil
coarse salt and freshly ground
black pepper
1 tablespoon olive oil, plus extra
for brushing the dish
1 leek, finely chopped
3 garlic cloves, finely chopped
4 cups spinach
½ teaspoon freshly grated nutmeg
pinch of cayenne pepper
½ cup coconut milk
¼ teaspoon Dijon mustard
hot toast, to serve

METHOD

1 Preheat the oven to 400°F.

2 Gently clean the mushrooms with paper towels. Remove and discard the stalks. Rub the underside of each mushroom with the extra virgin olive oil and season both sides with coarse salt and pepper. Place the mushrooms in a baking dish lightly brushed with a little olive oil.

3 Heat the olive oil in a pan. Add the leek, season, and gently cook until soft. Add the garlic to the pan. Cook gently for several minutes.

4 Stir in the spinach, nutmeg, and cayenne. Season and cook until the spinach wilts.

5 Finally, stir in the coconut milk and mustard, season generously, and gently heat through until the sauce reduces—about 5 to 10 minutes.

6 Fill each mushroom with the creamy spinach filling and bake in the oven for 25 to 30 minutes. Serve immediately with hot toast.

~ simple ~
SCRAMBLED TOFU

serves 2

Scrambled egg was always a winning dish on my morning weekend menu, so I won't deny I was a little sad to let it go when I opted for a vegan lifestyle. Little did I know there'd be a perfect replacement for my previously favorite protein-filled breakfast dish… and, truthfully, I now prefer it to the eggy original. I must admit I was more than a little dubious myself (beancurd? For breakfast?), because, as we all know, this "love it or hate it" ingredient needs a significant helping hand in the flavor department. However, fear not: all bases are covered here, resulting in a terrific alternative to traditional scrambled eggs! If you're resolutely in the "I'd rather eat my own sock camp" (I too was once of the same sentiment), I suggest you put those tofu reservations to one side until you at least try a mouthful for yourself—you may just be in for a scramble surprise.

INGREDIENTS

14oz firm tofu
1 tablespoon olive oil
2 scallions, sliced
salt and freshly ground black
pepper
1 teaspoon mild curry powder
1 teaspoon cider vinegar
1 tablespoon lemon juice
3 cups baby spinach
freshly chopped flat-leaf parsley,
to garnish
hot toast, to serve

METHOD

1 Drain the tofu and place it in a shallow bowl. Place a plate on top of it. Now place 2 × 14oz food cans (or similar) on top of the plate to weight it down. Set aside for 15 minutes, then drain the tofu once more to get rid of any excess liquid.

2 Heat the oil in a medium, non-stick frying pan. Add the scallions to the pan along with a little salt and pepper. When the onions begin to soften, crumble in the tofu.

3 Cook for a few minutes over medium heat before sprinkling in the curry powder. Stir to coat the tofu and pour in the cider vinegar and lemon juice. Season and cook for another 5 to 10 minutes.

4 Finally add the spinach and allow it to wilt a little before seasoning again. Garnish with freshly chopped flat-leaf parsley and serve with toast.

savory PUDLA PANCAKE

serves 2 to 4

Breakfast is probably the trickiest meal of the day for vegans and, as much as you might resist, you can often find yourself falling into a rut. I'm as guilty as the next person when it comes to maxing out oatmeal for weeks on end; however, once you've added this glorious chickpea-flour pancake recipe to your repertoire, breakfast, and indeed brunch, suddenly become that little bit more exciting. We can thank the vegetarian Mecca that is India for this one, although I have put my own little spin on it by creating one large thick pancake instead of several smaller ones. I like to think of it as an Indian pizza of sorts, as it can be sliced and served in the same way. With endless filling possibilities, this über easy batter is simply a base on which to build the breakfast of your plant-based dreams. So go forth and make pudla!

INGREDIENTS

1¾ cups gram (chickpea) flour
¼ teaspoon baking powder
¼ teaspoon ground cumin
¼ teaspoon paprika
pinch of cayenne pepper
pinch of dried chile flakes
1 teaspoon sea salt
½ teaspoon freshly ground
black pepper
juice of 1 lemon
3 to 4 tablespoons sunflower oil
¼ cup cooked peas
¼ cup cooked sweet corn
1 scallion, finely chopped
1 tablespoon freshly
chopped cilantro

METHOD

1 Place the gram flour in a large bowl along with the baking powder, spices, salt, and pepper. Lightly mix with a spatula to disperse the ingredients.

2 Add ½ cup water and the lemon juice and whisk into a thick batter.

3 Heat the oil in a 10 to 12in non-stick frying pan over low-to-medium heat —the pancake should cook relatively slowly.

4 Stir the peas, sweet corn, scallions, and cilantro into the batter. Add the batter to the pan in one go, spreading it out with a spatula until it reaches the edges.

5 Gently cook for around 10 minutes or until it is golden before carefully turning over and cooking for another 5 to 7 minutes on the other side.

6 Serve the thick, dense pancake cut into slices or quartered.

VEGETABLE RÖSTI
with a smoky roasted salsa
serves 2 to 4

Breakfast? Appetizer? Snack? You decide, but whichever you opt for, this easy-peasy rösti recipe is a great way of getting your fried-food fix without resorting to deep-frying. The crunchy exterior makes this seem much more naughty than it actually is, and the smoky roasted salsa gives it two thumbs up from me.

INGREDIENTS

For the salsa
1 cup cherry tomatoes, halved
salt and freshly ground
black pepper
½ teaspoon brown sugar
1 tablespoon balsamic vinegar
2 tablespoons extra virgin olive oil
2 roasted red bell peppers from a jar, drained and roughly chopped
1 red chile, seeded if preferred, and roughly chopped
1 garlic clove, roughly chopped
½ teaspoon smoked paprika

For the rösti
1 large zucchini, grated
1 large carrot, grated
1 baking potato, grated
pinch of white pepper
¼ teaspoon garlic powder
juice of ½ lemon
2 tablespoons olive oil
freshly chopped flat-leaf parsley, to garnish

METHOD

1 Preheat the oven to 400°F.

2 Place the tomatoes on a baking sheet. Season, sprinkle with the sugar, and drizzle with the balsamic vinegar and half the oil. Roast in the oven for 20 minutes and set aside to cool.

3 Place the tomatoes, red bell peppers, chile, garlic, and smoked paprika into a blender along with the remaining oil, season, and blend to a coarse sauce.

4 Place the grated vegetables in the center of a clean kitchen towel, pull the edges together, and squeeze out all the excess liquid from the vegetables. Place in a large bowl and stir in the white pepper, garlic powder, lemon juice, and 1 tablespoon of the oil. Stir well to incorporate.

5 Heat the remaining oil in a medium pan. Shape the vegetable mixture into individual patties using your hands and add to the pan. Cook over medium heat for 5 to 10 minutes or until they begin to brown on the underside, lifting gently with a spatula to check. Carefully flip over the röstis to cook on the other side.

6 Once they have browned on the other side (this will take another 5 to 10 minutes), serve hot with the salsa and a sprinkling of freshly chopped parsley.

super green
SMOOTHIE

serves 2

For those of you who are recoiling in horror at the thought of kale in a smoothie, let me first say I know exactly how you feel. In fact, it took quite a bit of courage before I mustered up the will even to try it, but when I eventually did—boy, was I surprised. Leafy? Actually, not really. A tad bitter? Pretty much the opposite. The balance between the fruit and vegetables is just right, making this an addictive morning option that will get your day off to a great start.

INGREDIENTS

1½ cups kale, chopped, hard
stalks removed
1 celery rib, chopped
3in piece of cucumber, peeled
and seeded
2 apples, peeled, cored, and
chopped
3 medjool dates, pitted
1 teaspoon ground cinnamon
juice of 1 lime
juice of ½ lemon
3 to 4 ice cubes, plus extra to serve

METHOD

1 Place all the ingredients in a blender. Add ¾ cup cold water and blend until completely smooth (this may take a while), adding a little more water if necessary.

2 Divide equally between two tall glasses and serve with lots of ice.

MIDDAY Meals & SIMPLE SUPPERS

GAZPACHO SHOTS

WHOLESOME MINESTRONE

ARUGULA SOUP WITH ROASTED
GARLIC BAGUETTE

SUPER-FAST BROCCOLI SOUP

SWEET POTATO AND KIWI SOUP

LIGHTLY SPICED LENTIL SOUP

SILKY-SMOOTH BLACK BEAN SOUP

WINTER SQUASH AND
COUSCOUS SALAD

FAVA BEAN FRITTERS WITH A TANGY
CUCUMBER SALAD

BUDDHA BOWL PARCELS

SWEET-AND-SOUR MARINATED TOFU

ZUCCHINI AND CANNELLINI
BEAN PATTIES

ROASTED SQUASH WITH A
CRUNCHY QUINOA FILLING

STUFFED MUSHROOM BURGERS AND
DIJON-COATED POTATO WEDGES

SPLIT PEA DHAL WITH FLATBREADS

CHANA MASALA

HOLE MOLE BLACK BEAN CHILI

POTATO AND CAULIFLOWER CURRY

CHEAT'S MOUSSAKA

WEEKNIGHT NOODLE STIR-FRY

BASIC GNOCCHI

PEARL BARLEY RISOTTO WITH
GLAZED BALSAMIC ROOT
VEGETABLES

PEA AND LEMON RISOTTO WITH
A MINT OIL DRIZZLE

TORTILLA PIZZAS

THICK-CRUST MUSHROOM PIZZA

SANTORINI-STYLE SPAGHETTI WITH
LEMON, CAPERS, AND TOMATOES

MACARO-NO CHEESE WITH
CRISPY KALE

SIMPLE HERB PASTA WITH
SLOW-ROASTED TOMATOES

GAZPACHO
～ shots ～

serves 6 to 8

My love for soup even extends to the cold variety, and in that (often maligned) category there is none so perfect as gazpacho. Whether you're a fan of this Spanish favorite or are ever so slightly perturbed at the thought of eating a meal that consists of cold puréed vegetables, let me assure you that this harmonious combination of ingredients is nothing less than summertime nectar. I like to serve it up *amuse bouche*-style in espresso cups or shot glasses… just enough to whet your appetite for whatever else your menu has in store.

INGREDIENTS

5 large tomatoes
2 slices stale good-quality white bread, crusts removed
½ green bell pepper, roughly chopped
1 small celery rib, roughly chopped
2 scallions, roughly chopped
⅓ cucumber, peeled and cut into chunks
1 garlic clove
1 tablespoon red wine vinegar
salt and freshly ground black pepper
¼ cup extra virgin olive oil

METHOD

1 Cover the tomatoes in freshly boiled water and set aside for several minutes. Drain, then peel, chop, and seed the tomatoes.

2 Soak the bread in a shallow bowlful of water.

3 Place the peeled tomatoes, green bell pepper, celery, scallions, cucumber, garlic, and red wine vinegar in a blender. Season with salt and pepper and blend until smooth.

4 Squeeze any excess water out of the bread and add to the blender along with the extra virgin olive oil. Blend until completely smooth and refrigerate for several hours.

5 Serve in small shot glasses or bowls.

TIP

Top with finely diced green bell pepper, cucumber, olives, and a generous drizzle of extra virgin olive oil for a final tasty flourish.

～ wholesome ～ MINESTRONE

serves 2 to 4

I often have a pan of this warming minestrone bubbling away on the stove. Full of goodness, this pasta-filled broth is a cinch to cook and works for either a casual lunch or hearty dinner… and it always seems to taste particularly good when reheated the next day. You can interchange the bean and pasta shapes, although I favor the borlotti bean and conchigliette combo. *Buon appetito!*

INGREDIENTS

1 tablespoon olive oil
1 onion, roughly chopped
1 celery rib, roughly chopped
1 carrot, roughly chopped
1 teaspoon dried oregano
salt and freshly ground
black pepper
2 garlic cloves, finely chopped
1 tablespoon red wine vinegar
1 × 14oz can chopped tomatoes
2 cups kale, roughly chopped
1 vegetable bouillon cube
1 × 14oz can borlotti beans,
drained and rinsed
1 cup small pasta shapes, such
as conchigliette
torn basil leaves and extra virgin
olive oil, to garnish

METHOD

1 Heat the oil in a large, heavy-bottomed saucepan and add the onion, celery, and carrot along with the oregano. Season with salt and pepper and sauté for several minutes until the vegetables begin to soften.

2 Add the garlic and cook over low heat for 1 to 2 minutes, ensuring it doesn't brown. Add the red wine vinegar and let it evaporate before pouring in the chopped tomatoes. Add the kale, crumble in the bouillon cube, add enough cold water to fill the pan, and simmer for 40 minutes.

3 When the volume has reduced, add the beans and pasta to the soup. Simmer for 7 to 10 minutes until the pasta is cooked through. Taste for seasoning. Garnish with the torn basil and a drizzle of extra virgin olive oil.

TIP

Serve with a dash of vegan pesto instead of the basil and olive oil to add a certain something to this already very Italian offering.

ARUGULA SOUP
with roasted garlic baguette
serves 2

Soup is a regular on my weekly menu. This arugula soup is perfectly uncomplicated, rendering the roasted garlic baguette the most time-consuming element of this dish… unless you wish to forgo it completely, of course. But if you're anything like me, you'll really want a hunk of garlic-infused carbohydrate to dunk into your bowl of green, plus it comes in handy when you want to mop up any soupy remnants.

INGREDIENTS

For the roasted garlic baguette
1 garlic bulb
1 tablespoon olive oil
1 small whole-grain baguette
1 small bunch fresh flat-leaf
parsley, finely chopped
10 tablespoons vegan butter
salt and freshly ground
black pepper

For the soup
1 tablespoon olive oil
6 shallots, thinly sliced
2 medium waxy potatoes, such as
Yukon Gold, peeled and diced
1 vegetable bouillon cube
8oz arugula

METHOD

1 Preheat the oven to 350°F. Place the whole garlic bulb in the center of a piece of foil, drizzle with the olive oil, and bake in the oven for an hour or until soft—the garlic cloves should yield easily to the touch.

2 Partially slice the baguette, making sure to leave it attached at the base of each slice and leaving enough room to pop the butter in between the slices.

3 Remove the garlic from the oven. Peel about 6 of the garlic cloves and mash with the back of a fork. Place the garlic, parsley, and butter in a bowl, season with salt and pepper, and mix to combine. Cover and chill for 30 minutes.

4 Divide the garlic butter mixture between the slices in the baguette. Place the loaf on a baking sheet and bake for 10 to 15 minutes.

5 For the soup, heat the oil in a large saucepan, add the shallots, and gently soften for 5 to 10 minutes, stirring to ensure they don't brown.

6 Add the potatoes to the pan, season, and stir. Crumble in the bouillon cube and add 3 cups freshly boiled water. Simmer for 15 minutes.

7 Add the arugula (reserving a few leaves) and allow to wilt. Transfer to a blender or food processor and blend until the soup is completely smooth. Return the soup to the pan and gently heat—do not allow it to boil. Season, garnish with the reserved arugula leaves, and serve with the garlic baguette.

～ super-fast ～
BROCCOLI SOUP

serves 2

Lunchtime pretty much always equals soup in my world. Even during the height of summer I just cannot help myself, which has forced me to come up with quick ways to satisfy my need for something hot and soothing midday, every day. While most hearty broths benefit from a significant time simmering on the stove, this simple soup is actually one of the few dishes that benefit from less cooking time—overcooked broccoli is never a pleasant experience and we don't want this to have a leftover Sunday-dinner flavor. Omit the cream if you wish, but be sure to return the blended soup to the pan for a few minutes so it can thicken and become lusciously smooth.

INGREDIENTS

1 tablespoon sunflower oil
1 small onion, finely chopped
1 celery rib, finely chopped
1 broccoli head (about 1lb 2oz), broken into small florets and stalk finely chopped
salt and freshly ground black pepper
1 scant teaspoon cider vinegar
1 teaspoon vegetable stock granules or ½ vegetable bouillon cube
¼ cup soy milk or soy cream

METHOD

1 Heat the oil in a medium, heavy-bottomed pan. Add the onion, celery, and chopped broccoli stalk to the pan. Season with salt and pepper, add the cider vinegar, and gently sweat for several minutes until the vegetables begin to soften.

2 Add the broccoli florets to the pan and pour in enough freshly boiled water to just cover the broccoli and no more. Stir in the vegetable stock granules or cube and allow to dissolve before simmering for 5 minutes or until the broccoli has cooked through.

3 Transfer to a blender and process until smooth.

4 Return to the pan, add the soy milk or cream, and gently heat. Taste for seasoning and serve.

sweet potato and KIWI SOUP

serves 2 to 4

Fruit in soup? Have I gone completely mad?! Perhaps so, but I'll be darned if this combination doesn't, for some reason unbeknownst to me, sing. Rightly or wrongly I added a kiwi and now I can't make this meal without one—I had one lying forlornly in a fruit bowl once and I just decided to give it an impromptu soupy home. Luckily, it enhanced the whole affair, giving it an understated "zing," but be careful not to go overboard or you may interfere with the fruit/veggie equilibrium we have going here—and that will only spell disaster.

INGREDIENTS

1 tablespoon olive oil

4 to 5 garlic cloves, roughly chopped

3 small to medium sweet potatoes (about 1¼lb), peeled and roughly chopped (peelings reserved for Sweet Potato Chips, see Tip)

salt and freshly ground black pepper

1 tablespoon vegetable stock granules or 1 vegetable bouillon cube

1 kiwi fruit, peeled and roughly chopped

METHOD

1 Heat the oil in a large, heavy-bottomed saucepan. Add the garlic and cook over low heat for 1 to 2 minutes, ensuring it doesn't brown.

2 Add the sweet potatoes, season generously with salt and pepper, and stir. Cook for a few minutes before covering with water and stirring in the stock granules or crumbling in the bouillon cube. Bring to a simmer and cover, allowing the sweet potato to cook gently and soften for about 10 to 15 minutes.

3 Transfer to a blender, add the kiwi, and process until completely smooth. Return the soup to the pan, add some filtered water if it seems too thick, and let it warm through over very low heat. Taste for seasoning and serve with Sweet Potato Chips (see Tip).

TIP

Place the sweet potato peelings in a roasting pan. Coat with 1 tablespoon olive oil and 1 teaspoon smoked paprika. Season and bake for 15 to 20 minutes at 400°F. *Voilà*, Sweet Potato Chips!

lightly spiced LENTIL SOUP

serves 4

I have a serious weakness for red lentils. Earthy, rich, and endlessly satisfying, they can be used in soups, stews, and even baked pasta—just see my Red Lentil and Spinach Lasagna (page 96) for proof. They take particularly well to spices too and, along with the addition of creamy coconut milk, can be easily transformed from a simple legume into an unctuous meal teeming with flavor and bite. I prefer to let the patient simmering do all the hard work here, but if your preference is for a super smooth texture then by all means use a hand-held blender at the end… either way will warrant a double thumbs-up.

INGREDIENTS

1 tablespoon sunflower oil
(or 1 teaspoon coconut oil)
1 red onion, finely chopped
salt and freshly ground
black pepper
1 red chile, seeded
1 clove garlic, crushed
thumb-size piece of ginger
1 cup dried red lentils
1 teaspoon ground coriander
1 teaspoon paprika
1 teaspoon cumin
1 × 14oz can coconut milk
1 vegetable bouillon cube
juice of 1 lime
fresh cilantro leaves, to garnish

METHOD

1 Heat the oil in a medium, heavy-bottomed saucepan. Add the onion, season with salt and pepper, cover, and gently soften for several minutes.

2 Meanwhile, finely chop the chile, garlic, and ginger together. Add to pan, cover, and cook for a few more minutes until the flavors begin to infuse.

3 Rinse the red lentils and add to pan along with the ground coriander, paprika, and cumin. Mix thoroughly and then pour in the coconut milk and 3 cups water. Crumble in the vegetable bouillon cube and lightly season with salt and pepper.

4 Cover, bring to a boil, and then lower to a gentle simmer for forty minutes, ensuring to stir frequently.

5 Once the lentils have softened and disintegrated to form a thick, creamy soup, take off the heat, pour in the lime juice, taste for seasoning, and serve with a few fresh cilantro leaves for garnish. Alternatively, for a thinner texture, you could use a hand-held blender prior to serving.

~ silky-smooth ~
BLACK BEAN SOUP

serves 2 to 4

This black bean wonder is enough to smash any ideas of soup being somewhat dull and predictable. Yes, in essence, it's just puréed beans with a little added zip (gotta love that lime!), but something happens when all those flavors come together to create this simple yet standout appetizer for your ultimate Mexican meal—nothing precedes enchiladas or tacos (page 99) like a steaming bowl of black bean soup, trust me. *Arriba!*

INGREDIENTS

1 tablespoon olive oil
1 onion, finely chopped
1 red bell pepper, finely chopped
salt and freshly ground
black pepper
1 red chile, seeded and finely
chopped
2 garlic cloves, finely chopped
1 heaping teaspoon smoked paprika
1 teaspoon ground cumin
½ teaspoon dried oregano
2 × 14oz cans black beans
2 sprigs thyme
1 heaping teaspoon vegetable
stock granules
1 teaspoon balsamic vinegar
or vegan Worcestershire sauce
juice of 1 lime

To serve
1 avocado, roughly chopped
handful of chopped cilantro
juice of ½ lime

METHOD

1 Heat the oil in a large, heavy-bottomed saucepan. Add the onion and red bell pepper, season with salt and pepper, and lightly sauté for a few minutes until the vegetables begin to soften. Stir frequently.

2 Add the chile and garlic and lightly cook for a few minutes before adding the smoked paprika, cumin, and oregano. Sweat for several minutes, allowing the flavors of the spices to infuse.

3 Drain and rinse the black beans and add to the pan. Thoroughly coat the beans in all the spices before adding the thyme and vegetable stock granules. Then pour in just enough water to cover the beans.

4 Add the balsamic vinegar or Worcestershire sauce and simmer for about 20 minutes.

5 Transfer to a blender, add the lime juice, and process until completely smooth. Return to the pan and gently heat, adding a little more water if necessary. Season to taste.

6 Ladle into bowls and top with the avocado, cilantro and a squeeze of fresh lime before serving.

WINTER SQUASH
and couscous salad

serves 2 to 4

Call me crazy, but I like to think of this as a semi-virtuous winter salad. When you're surrounded by calorie-laden comfort food yet can't face lettuce and dressing, this is the dish to satisfy those cravings without the often ensuing guilt. The sage and rosemary are crucial in making this recipe seasonally apt (I do try!), with the lightly toasted almonds lending some much-needed crunch—for me, texture in vegan food is the key to a winning dish, and this one succeeds on all fronts. As a side or on its own, it's a super-easy option when those early evenings start to creep in, and means you can settle down to your television safe in the knowledge that your couch-potato ways are somewhat negated by this healthy evening meal. Well, sorta.

INGREDIENTS

1 squash (about 1lb 2oz), peeled, halved, seeded, and cut into small chunks
2 tablespoons sunflower oil
1 sprig rosemary, leaves finely chopped
1 tablespoon finely chopped fresh sage
sea salt and freshly ground black pepper
1½ cups couscous
1½ cups frozen peas
½ cup sliced almonds, toasted
3 tablespoons extra virgin olive oil

METHOD

1 Preheat the oven to 400°F.

2 Place the squash in a roasting pan, drizzle in the sunflower oil, sprinkle with the herbs, and season well with salt and pepper. Roast in the oven for 1 hour or until completely soft. Turn the oven off but leave the squash in the oven until needed.

3 Soak the couscous in an equal volume of freshly boiled water, cover, and let stand for 10 minutes to absorb the liquid before fluffing with a fork.

4 Defrost the peas by covering them with freshly boiled water, leave for 5 minutes, and then drain.

5 Remove the roasted squash from the oven and stir in the couscous, peas, almonds, and extra virgin olive oil. Season to taste and serve warm.

FAVA BEAN FRITTERS
with a tangy cucumber salad

serves 2 to 3

Since visiting Palestine in my teens, I've been a tad obsessed with falafel, hummus, and pita—coming from a small Irish town I found these flavors transformational for my relatively uninformed palate, and the gateway to my life-long love affair with food. These fritters were a happy accident in my bid to perfect the fava bean falafel (just like the ones I had tasted in Bethlehem all those years ago), but are more akin to a takeout pea fritter than a Middle Eastern snack (what can I say?—a marriage of two cultures I equally adore!).

INGREDIENTS

For the quick-pickled cucumber
1 cucumber, peeled and very thinly sliced
2 teaspoons sugar
3 to 4 tablespoons white wine vinegar
1 tablespoon chopped dill

1⅓ cups frozen fava beans
½ onion, roughly chopped
1 garlic clove
1 teaspoon ground cumin
¼ teaspoon cayenne pepper
1 teaspoon baking powder
1 tablespoon all-purpose flour, plus several extra tablespoons to coat
juice of ½ lemon or lime
salt and freshly ground black pepper
sunflower oil, for shallow-frying
pita bread, hummus, salad, and chili sauce, to serve

METHOD

1 First, make the pickled cucumber. Place the cucumber in a shallow bowl. Sprinkle with the sugar and pour in the vinegar. Stir, cover, and chill.

2 Place the fava beans in a large bowl and cover with freshly boiled water. Once they have defrosted, drain and peel them. Transfer to a food processor. Add the onion along with the garlic, cumin, cayenne, baking powder, flour, and the lemon or lime juice, season with salt and pepper, and blend.

3 Take a heaping teaspoon of the mixture, roll into a ball, and then flatten into a thick patty shape. You should get approximately 10 balls from the mix. Coat each patty in flour and place on a baking sheet lined with parchment paper. Chill for 30 minutes.

4 Preheat the oven to 300°F. Give the patties another coating of flour just before frying. Pour about ¾in of the oil into a small, non-stick, heavy-bottomed frying pan. When the oil is hot, gently add several fritters at a time. Fry until golden and crispy on one side before turning over and cooking on the other side—7 to 10 minutes on each side. Place the cooked patties on a baking sheet and keep hot in the oven while you fry the remainder.

5 Remove the pickled cucumber from the fridge and stir in the chopped dill. Serve the fritters warm, 3 to 4 in each fresh pita bread with hummus, salad, quick-pickled cucumber, and chili sauce.

∽ buddha bowl ᴄ
PARCELS

serves 2

This is my spin on every vegan's favorite standby meal… the almighty Buddha Bowl. If you're not quite familiar with the Buddha Bowl, let me direct you to the wiki explanation of *Oryoki* (the Japanese practice from which it originates) that essentially describes it as a "meditative form of eating." That is, take some healthful veggies, cook then gently, plop 'em in a bowl, and eat until you're satisfied but not totally overstuffed—sounds perfectly zen to me! I tend to make it when I'm juggling a thousand things, because you can pop it in the oven and forget about it for an hour—oh, and it happens to taste amazing too. With no salt and pepper (and you can omit or swap the soy sauce if you so wish), this is my idea of Buddhist-induced bliss in food form; even if it does make me feel a wee bit hippy-dippy when I'm eating it. Altogether now, "Om"…

INGREDIENTS

2 large sweet potatoes,
roughly chopped
1 onion, roughly chopped
1 red bell pepper, roughly chopped
2 garlic cloves, finely sliced
2 tablespoons soy sauce
2 tablespoons sushi seasoning
or rice wine vinegar
2 tablespoons sesame oil
2 teaspoons Tabasco sauce
1½ cups kale, torn into small pieces

For the brown rice
½ cup brown rice
1 lemon
2 cardamom pods
3 to 4 cloves
1 star anise

METHOD

1 Preheat the oven to 400°F. Tear off 2 large sheets of foil measuring about 12 × 16cm.

2 Divide the sweet potatoes between the foil sheets and top with the onion, bell pepper, and garlic. Fold the foil around the vegetables, leaving an opening at the top.

3 Divide the soy sauce, sushi seasoning, sesame oil, and Tabasco sauce between each parcel and place half the kale into the top of each. Seal the parcels, place on a baking sheet, and cook in the oven for 1 hour.

4 Place the rice in a medium pan with 1 cup water. Using a vegetable peeler, remove the lemon peel in thick strips and add to the rice with the cardamom pods, cloves, and star anise. Bring to a boil before turning down to a simmer. The rice is ready when all the water has been completely absorbed, after about 50 minutes. Remove the peel and spices, fluff the rice with a fork, and place in a bowl. Remove the Buddha Bowl parcels from the oven, open carefully, and pour the contents over the cooked rice to serve.

sweet-and-sour
MARINATED TOFU

serves 4

Forget everything you think you know about tofu because this unctuous marinated version is deliciously tasty proof that this much-maligned ingredient can be anything but flavorless and boring. The key here is to drain as much liquid from the block of tofu as possible—after that, it's a case of allowing the marinade to do its thing. The crispy caramelized outer and firm texture gives this dish real impact and I doubt anyone will be complaining when you serve it as the main event for dinner. The time to make peace with tofu has officially arrived.

INGREDIENTS

14oz firm tofu
¼ cup miso paste
juice of 1 lime
2 tablespoons tamari
2 tablespoons sesame oil
2 tablespoons agave nectar
or maple syrup
¼ cup peanut, sunflower,
or canola oil

TIP

If you're really short of time, 15 minutes' marinating will suffice—just!

METHOD

1 Drain the tofu and place it in a shallow bowl with a plate on top. Now put two 14oz food cans (or similar) on top of the plate to weight it down, and set aside for 15 minutes.

2 Drain the excess liquid, pat dry, and cut lengthwise to form two equal halves. Then slice each half into two triangles, to give you four triangles in total. Return the tofu to the shallow bowl.

3 In a bowl, whisk together the miso paste, lime juice, tamari, sesame oil, and agave or maple syrup. Pour the marinade over the tofu and turn the tofu several times to ensure it is completely coated. Set aside for at least 1 hour— the longer you leave it, the better.

4 Heat the oil in a medium, non-stick, heavy-bottomed frying pan and add the tofu. Fry over medium heat until dark and caramelized on one side (about 10 minutes) before turning over and doing the same on the other side.

5 Serve the tofu hot or cold with a Green Bean Salad with Lemon, Garlic, and Chile (see page 131).

zucchini and cannellini
BEAN PATTIES

serves 4

Bean burgers can be fragile, messy things that come apart easily and have a habit of crumbling. I've attempted to avoid the obvious pitfalls by adding some grated zucchini, which not only strengthens the patty shape but also gives it some much-needed texture… something to really sink your teeth into. Now, normally I wouldn't be so insistent on a specific ingredient (I am the queen of "make do" myself); however, I really feel the polenta is a necessary addition here in giving the exterior that perfect crispy crunch. Whichever way you choose to eat the burgers (bun or not), you'll be grateful for that added bit of bite.

INGREDIENTS

2 × 14oz cans cannellini beans,
drained and rinsed
salt and freshly ground
white pepper
1 zucchini
1 tablespoon sunflower oil,
plus ¼ cup extra for
shallow-frying
3 scallions, chopped
1 garlic clove, finely chopped
1 teaspoon cider vinegar
¾ cup fresh flat-leaf parsley,
roughly chopped
1 tablespoon all-purpose flour
1 tablespoon polenta,
plus 2 to 3 tablespoons to coat
side salad or burger buns, to serve

METHOD

1 Place the beans in a large bowl, season generously with salt and pepper, and mash into a coarse paste, leaving some beans whole.

2 Grate the zucchini, place it in a clean kitchen towel, and squeeze out any excess liquid. Heat 1 tablespoon of the oil in a frying pan, add the scallions, garlic, and cider vinegar, and cook for a few minutes until soft.

3 Add the raw grated zucchini to the mashed beans along with the scallion mixture, season generously, and combine using a spatula. Add the parsley, flour, 1 tablespoon of the polenta, and season. Mix thoroughly, adding a little more polenta if the mixture is still quite sticky.

4 Divide the mixture into 4 equal portions and roll each into a ball. Flatten gently to create a burger shape, ensuring there are no cracks around the edges. Place 2 tablespoons of the polenta in a shallow bowl and coat each burger in it. Place the burgers on a baking sheet lined with parchment paper. Chill for 1 hour.

5 Heat the ¼ cup oil in a large, non-stick, heavy-bottomed pan over medium heat and add the burgers. Cook for 10 minutes on each side until golden and crunchy. Serve with a side salad or in a burger bun.

ROASTED SQUASH
with a crunchy quinoa filling

serves 2

There are limitless ways to serve roasted squash and I have a lot of fun playing around with different combinations. I always seem to return to quinoa, however, because it provides such great balance to the vegan plate. Packed full of protein, as well as host of other nutrients, it really is a powerhouse of a grain and goes with just about anything. I like the crunch the almonds and pumpkin seeds provide here (which will certainly banish any texture qualms you may have) and the tangy maple dressing does a fine job of lifting all those dormant flavors off your plate, making this a terrific option for any occasion.

INGREDIENTS

1 large butternut squash (about
1½lb), halved, seeded, and scored
2 tablespoons vegan butter or oil
salt and freshly ground
black pepper

For the quinoa filling
1½ cups quinoa
2 scallions, finely sliced
¾ cup sliced almonds
¾ cup pumpkin seeds
⅓ cup golden raisins
¾ cup fresh cilantro, chopped

For the dressing
1 teaspoon Dijon mustard
juice of 1 lime
2 tablespoons maple syrup
1 tablespoon red wine vinegar
2½ tablespoons olive oil

METHOD

1 Preheat the oven to 350°F.

2 Place the butternut halves, cut side up, in a roasting pan. Spread half the butter or drizzle the oil over each butternut squash half, season with salt and pepper, and bake in the oven for 40 to 50 minutes until soft. Occasionally brush the butter and juices over the squash halves so they don't dry out.

3 Cook the quinoa according to the package instructions. Fluff with a fork, cover, and set aside.

4 Put all the dressing ingredients with some seasoning in a lidded screwtop jar and shake well until they emulsify.

5 Mix the scallions into the quinoa along with half of the dressing. Stir in the almonds, pumpkin seeds, and golden raisins, along with most of the chopped cilantro.

6 Stuff each squash half with half of the filling. Drizzle with the remaining dressing and garnish with the rest of the chopped cilantro before serving.

STUFFED MUSHROOM BURGERS
and dijon – coated potato wedges

serves 4

There's no reason to do without burger and fries when meat is no longer on the menu. By stuffing the already "meaty" portobello mushrooms, you create a dense texture that would fool anyone into thinking there's more than just veggies inside that bun—and when I first turned vegan, that was of paramount importance. I was never a fully fledged fast-food aficionado, but I enjoyed the occasional blowout. Now, however, I can indulge my greasy whims from the comfort of my home and without harming any unsuspecting cows in the process! It's diner food without the moral, calorific, and overly-processed dilemma, and who could ask for more than that?

INGREDIENTS

For the ketchup
4 tomatoes, halved
salt and freshly ground black pepper
½ teaspoon ground allspice
1 tablespoon balsamic vinegar
1 teaspoon brown sugar
1 tablespoon olive oil

For the wedges
4 large potatoes, washed
2 teaspoons Dijon mustard
2 tablespoons oil
1 teaspoon cider vinegar
1 sprig rosemary, leaves chopped

For the mushroom burgers
1 tablespoon olive oil, plus extra
for greasing
4 tablespoons vegan butter
or margarine
½ onion, finely diced
4 portobello mushrooms

METHOD

1 Preheat the oven to 400°F.

2 Place the tomatoes on a baking sheet. Sprinkle with 1 teaspoon each of salt and pepper, the allspice, balsamic vinegar, brown sugar, and oil and roast for 1 hour. Remove from the oven and set aside to cool before pressing through a sieve. Season and chill until needed—the ketchup will keep for two days.

3 Slice the potatoes into thick wedges and place in a roasting pan. Whisk together the Dijon mustard, oil, cider vinegar, rosemary, 1 teaspoon salt, and some freshly ground black pepper. Pour the mixture over the wedges and toss to coat thoroughly. Roast for 1 hour, shaking the pan occasionally so the wedges don't stick. Season again when they are removed from the oven.

4 For the mushroom burger stuffing, heat the oil and half of the vegan butter or margarine in a medium-sized, non-stick, heavy-bottomed frying pan and add the onion. Season and sauté gently until it begins to soften. Remove the stalks from the portobello mushrooms, finely chop, and add to the pan. Sweat the onion and mushroom stalks for a minute or two before adding the garlic and thyme. Season generously and cook for a few more minutes.

5 Add the bread crumbs to the pan along with the remaining vegan butter or margarine and red wine vinegar. Let the bread crumbs fry for a few minutes until golden before finally adding the toasted pine nuts and freshly chopped parsley.

INGREDIENTS

1 garlic clove, finely chopped

1 sprig thyme, leaves chopped

1 cup white bread crumbs

1 tablespoon red wine vinegar

3 tablespoons pine nuts, toasted

¼ cup fresh flat-leaf parsley, chopped

4 ciabatta rolls, halved

arugula leaves, to serve

METHOD

6 Lightly grease a baking sheet. Rub the mushrooms with oil and season the outsides with salt and pepper. Divide the bread crumb mixture between them and pack it in tightly using the back of a spoon or your fingers. Place on the baking sheet and bake in the oven with the wedges for the last 30 minutes of their cooking time.

7 Spread a little ketchup in each roll and serve the burgers in them with a handful of arugula leaves and the potato wedges on the side.

SPLIT PEA DHAL
with flatbreads

serves 4

You could say that dhal has officially replaced mashed potatoes as my go-to comfort food meal. While there will always be a place in my heart for the humble potato, the unpleasant bloated feeling that often appears post-consumption has meant I am less and less inclined to eat it. This is where legumes step in, and the fact they pack a punch in the protein stakes means their substance unequivocally matches their style.

INGREDIENTS

For the dhal
1 tablespoon sunflower oil
1 small onion, finely chopped
salt and freshly ground
black pepper
2 garlic cloves, finely chopped
1¼in piece of fresh ginger, peeled
and finely chopped
1 red or green chile, seeded and
finely chopped
½ teaspoon ground turmeric
1 teaspoon ground cumin
1¼ cups yellow split peas, soaked
overnight, drained, and rinsed
1 vegetable bouillon cube

For the flatbreads
2 cups all-purpose flour, plus extra
for dusting
½ teaspoon active dry yeast
1 tablespoon olive oil, plus extra
for oiling

METHOD

1 First make the dhal. Heat the oil in a heavy-bottomed saucepan, add the onion along with a little salt and pepper, cover, and gently cook over medium heat for several minutes. Add the garlic, ginger, and chile, stir, and cook for 5 minutes. Add the turmeric and cumin, and cook for another 3 to 4 minutes.

2 Stir in the split peas and cover with water. Crumble in the bouillon cube and bring to a boil before turning down to a gentle simmer. Simmer for 1 to 1½ hours, stirring occasionally, until the peas are completely soft. You will need to add more water occasionally to loosen the mixture.

3 Meanwhile, make the bread. In a large bowl, mix the flour and yeast and season. Make a well in the center and pour in ¾ cup cold water and the oil. Using your hands, gradually work the flour into the water until a soft dough is formed, adding more flour if it's too sticky and a little more water if it's too dry. Turn onto a lightly floured surface and knead for 10 minutes. Oil a bowl and turn the dough into it. Cover and let sit for 10 minutes.

4 Heat a large, non-stick frying pan until it starts to smoke. Tear off a quarter of the dough and form into a flat, roundish shape with your hands. Place in the pan and cook for mere minutes before turning over to cook the other side. You'll know its ready when it starts to puff slightly and brown around the edges. Keep warm while you prepare and cook the remaining breads.

5 Taste the dhal for seasoning and serve with the flatbreads.

chana MASALA

serves 4

There are certain dishes I know like the back of my hand and this is emphatically one of them. Whenever I can't decide what to cook or don't have the energy to create something new, I always turn to my trusty Chana Masala to save the day. I even served this to friends just before we moved back to the UK because I only had one pot to work with—and we ate it from an assortment of makeshift bowls... I think that day I was "The Hostess with the Leastest." Literally. Now, I don't know about you, but in my experience no two Chana Masalas are the same, so this is my own personal version of a vegetarian Indian classic that will have you licking the plate (or makeshift bowl) clean and asking for more.

INGREDIENTS

2 tablespoons sunflower oil

1 onion, finely chopped

2 garlic cloves, finely chopped

1 in piece of fresh ginger, peeled and finely chopped

1 red chile, seeded and finely chopped

salt and freshly ground black pepper

1 heaping teaspoon garam masala

¼ teaspoon ground turmeric

¼ teaspoon brown sugar

1 × 14oz can chopped tomatoes

1 × 14oz can chickpeas, drained and rinsed

1¼ cups coconut milk

¾ cup fresh cilantro, chopped

basmati rice, to serve

METHOD

1 Heat the oil in a medium, heavy-bottomed pan and add the onion. Add the garlic, ginger, and chile to the pan along with some salt and pepper. Cook for several minutes until they begin to exude an aroma.

2 Sprinkle in the garam masala, turmeric, and a pinch of the sugar. Sauté for several minutes before adding the canned tomatoes, a little more salt and pepper, and the remaining sugar. Stir well and bring to a gentle simmer for around 20 minutes.

3 Add the chickpeas to the sauce. Pour in half the coconut milk, season again, and simmer for 5 to 10 minutes before adding the rest. Give the seasoning a final check and simmer for another 10 minutes. Stir in half of the chopped cilantro and serve with basmati rice, sprinkling the rest of the cilantro over the top.

hole mole
BLACK BEAN CHILI

serves 4 to 6

For some people, chili without meat just doesn't make sense (its full title is chili con carne after all). But because it's one of my favorite dishes to serve at parties, I had to find a way to overcome (and perhaps overcompensate for) the lack of flesh. Thankfully my hard work paid off and here's a gutsy chili to satisfy all tastes… in fact I've even seen some of my meat-fiend friends go back for seconds, thirds, and more.

INGREDIENTS

For the chili
1 tablespoon sunflower oil
1 large onion, very finely diced
salt and freshly ground black pepper
1 heaping teaspoon ground cumin
pinch of ground cinnamon
½ teaspoon chile powder
½ teaspoon dried chile flakes
1 teaspoon smoked paprika
pinch of cayenne pepper
1 red bell pepper, roughly chopped
1 yellow bell pepper,
roughly chopped
1 green bell pepper, roughly
chopped
1 red chile, seeded and chopped
3 garlic cloves, finely chopped
1 tablespoon tomato paste
1 × 14oz can chopped tomatoes
pinch of sugar
few drops of Tabasco sauce
1 tablespoon balsamic vinegar

METHOD

1 Heat the oil in a heavy-bottomed saucepan. Add the onion, season with salt and pepper, and let it soften for several minutes before adding the dried spices and sweating for a few minutes more. Add the bell peppers, season, cover, and cook together for at least 10 minutes or until softened before adding the chopped chile and garlic.

2 Stir in the tomato paste until everything is coated, then pour in the chopped tomatoes. Add the sugar, Tabasco, balsamic vinegar, and about ½ cup water. Season and stir to incorporate. Simmer for around 25 to 30 minutes, occasionally adding more water if the sauce becomes too dry.

3 Drain and rinse the beans. Add to the pan and simmer for another 15 to 20 minutes.

4 Meanwhile, divide each tortilla into 8 triangular pieces. Heat ⅔ cup of the oil in a large frying pan over medium heat. Lightly fry several of the tortilla pieces until golden before turning over and frying on the other side. Transfer to a plate lined with paper towels and season immediately with sea salt.

5 Repeat the process until all the pieces are golden and crunchy. You may need to add a little more oil about halfway through.

INGREDIENTS

2 × 14oz cans black beans
¾oz good-quality dark chocolate
(70 to 80 percent cocoa solids)
chopped fresh cilantro, sliced
avocado and lime wedges, to serve

For the tortilla chips
5 flour tortillas
⅔ cup to ¾ cup sunflower oil

METHOD

6 Just before serving, break the chocolate into small squares and stir into the chili. The sauce will turn thick and glossy. Allow everything to amalgamate before serving.

7 Serve the chili with chopped fresh cilantro, sliced avocado, wedges of lime for squeezing, and a stack of homemade tortilla chips.

MIDDAY MEALS & SIMPLE SUPPERS

potato and cauliflower CURRY

serves 4

A smidge saucier than your typical aloo gobi, this hearty Potato and Cauliflower Curry is a substantial dish with a robust, earthy appeal. Healthier than a visit to your local take-out, it'll fool you into thinking you're indulging when you're not—even with a decent dollop of dairy-free raita on top.

INGREDIENTS

1 tablespoon sunflower/coconut oil
1 onion, roughly chopped
½ fennel bulb, thinly sliced
salt and freshly ground black pepper
2 garlic cloves, finely chopped
1 large green chile, seeded and finely chopped
1 in piece of fresh ginger, peeled and finely chopped
2 to 3 medium potatoes, chopped
1 cauliflower, broken into florets
1 heaping teaspoon garam masala
1 scant teaspoon ground turmeric
½ teaspoon ground coriander
½ teaspoon ground allspice
½ teaspoon chile powder
1 tablespoon tomato paste
¾ cup tomato sauce
½ teaspoon sugar
1 vegetable bouillon cube
1½ cups cavolo nero or kale
¾ cup fresh cilantro, chopped
vegan raita (see page 135) and brown rice, to serve

METHOD

1 Heat the oil in a large, heavy-bottomed pan, add the onion and fennel, season with salt and pepper, and sweat for several minutes until they begin to soften.

2 Add the garlic, chile, and ginger to the pan. Stir to incorporate and cover tightly, allowing the flavors to infuse over low heat for several minutes.

3 Add the potatoes to the pan, cover, and cook for a few minutes before adding the cauliflower florets.

4 Sprinkle in the spices and stir well, ensuring the potato and cauliflower florets are completely coated. Cover and allow the spices to release their fragrant aroma before stirring through the tomato paste, sauce, sugar, and a splash of water. Season, cover, and cook for another minute or two.

5 Crumble in the vegetable bouillon cube and simmer for 30 to 40 minutes until the vegetables are just tender, adding more water if necessary. Make sure that the cauliflower doesn't overcook: it should retain its shape and texture.

6 Roughly chop the cavolo nero or kale and add to the pan in the final 10 minutes of cooking, allowing it to wilt. Taste for seasoning and add most of the chopped cilantro, retaining some for the garnish.

7 Serve with a dollop of raita, freshly boiled brown rice, and adorned with the remaining cilantro.

cheat's
MOUSSAKA

serves 4 to 6

I've paired this Greek-style moussaka down to the bare essentials in a bid to make a tiresomely complicated dish more straightforward (otherwise I'd be making it once a year instead of once a month), and if you're really organized you'll have some Two-Step Tomato Sauce stashed away in the freezer to make life even easier. Where I could easily have subbed the usual lamb with lentils, I've simply eliminated the unnecessary part and shined the focus on what I think are the best parts anyway… sliced potato and eggplant. I haven't forgotten the traditional cinnamon addition, and while I would normally insist on a cinnamon stick, in this case the ground variety actually works better. The dish might be pared down in content but definitely not in taste, which goes to prove that, despite what your teachers might've told you, cheating isn't always bad.

INGREDIENTS

3 large potatoes, sliced into
$^1/_8$in rounds
2 eggplants, sliced into
$^1/_4$in rounds
3 tablespoons olive oil
Double quantity of Two-Step
Tomato Sauce (see page 138) with
1 teaspoon ground cinnamon
added before simmering

For the easy white sauce
1$^1/_4$ cups soy milk
$^1/_2$ cup soy cream
1 tablespoon all-purpose flour
freshly grated nutmeg
salt and freshly ground
black pepper

METHOD

1 Preheat the oven to 350°F.

2 Bring a medium pan of salted water to a boil and blanch the potato slices for about 5 minutes, drain, and set aside.

3 Brush both sides of the eggplant slices with olive oil. Heat a grill pan and grill each round until soft and marked on both sides, adding a little more oil if necessary. Set the rounds aside until required.

4 Whisk all the easy white sauce ingredients together in a small, non-stick saucepan and bring to a gentle simmer, stirring continuously until it thickens.

5 To assemble the moussaka, spoon a layer of tomato sauce on the bottom of a 7in baking dish. Layer in half the eggplant slices, followed by half the potato slices, and season. Repeat the layers of tomato sauce and vegetables and top with the white sauce, spreading it over in an even layer.

6 Cover with foil and bake for 30 minutes. Bake uncovered for another 15 minutes. Let the moussaka cool slightly before serving with salad.

weeknight noodle STIR-FRY

serves 2

We all need super-quick options for those times when we're in a rush. The sweet chili addition might be a little less healthy than a homemade sauce, but I'm happy to lean on these store-bought products now and again for ease. I've tried to balance the bad with the good here, so go big on the kale. If you're really averse to the store-bought sauce, mash some chile, garlic, and ginger in a pestle and mortar for a similar result.

INGREDIENTS

For the sauce
2 tablespoons sweet chili sauce
(or 2 tablespoons sambal olek plus
1 teaspoon agave nectar)
juice of 1 lime
1 teaspoon cider vinegar
2 tablespoons soy sauce
1 teaspoon sesame oil
1 tablespoon oil

For the stir-fry
2 tablespoons peanut oil
3 scallions, finely sliced
1 carrot, sliced diagonally
6 to 8 baby sweet corn,
sliced diagonally
3 tablespoons soy sauce, plus extra
for seasoning
5½oz marinated tofu pieces
1½ cups kale, chopped
5½oz udon noodles
chopped cilantro and toasted
sesame or hemp seeds, to serve

METHOD

1 Bring a large pan of water to a boil for the noodles.

2 Whisk together all the sauce ingredients until they fully emulsify. Set aside until needed.

3 Heat the peanut oil in a wok or large frying pan. Add the scallions to the wok and cook until just starting to crisp up a little.

4 Add the carrot and sweet corn to the wok along with the soy sauce. Cook for several minutes until the vegetables begin to soften.

5 Toss in the marinated tofu. Stir-fry for several minutes before adding the kale. Add a small amount of the sauce and let the kale cook down.

6 Cook the udon noodles in the boiling water for 6 to 8 minutes. Drain, then rinse under cool water before adding to the wok along with the remaining sauce.

7 Stir to heat through, season with a little more soy sauce, and serve with some chopped cilantro and a sprinkling of toasted sesame seeds or hemp seeds.

~ basic ~
GNOCCHI

serves 2 to 3

This is the easiest gnocchi recipe you're likely to come across—I have a habit of stripping things back to the most basic steps. The trick is to try to create a workable dough with the least amount of flour possible, so while I've recommended ½ cup, that's the maximum amount you should use—but if the dough comes together with only three-quarters of that, great! It's also crucial that there are no lumps in the potatoes—if you have a potato ricer, definitely use that, otherwise press it through a sieve with the back of a spoon… not a step that can be missed, unfortunately. Where others recommend rolling the dough out into ropes and dividing them with a sharp knife, I like to tear off small pieces and roll them into bite-size balls.

INGREDIENTS

3 medium potatoes
(about 1lb 2oz), chopped into
medium chunks
salt and freshly ground
black pepper
½ cup all-purpose flour, plus extra
for dusting
Two-Step Tomato sauce (page 138)
or Pistachio, Parsley, and Walnut
Pesto (page 119), to serve

METHOD

1 Bring a medium pan of salted water to a boil, add the potato chunks, and cook until soft. Drain and mash the potatoes and then push through a potato ricer or sieve.

2 Season generously with salt and pepper and set aside to cool completely.

3 Sift half the flour into the mash and knead it in, adding more until a workable dough is formed.

4 Dust a worksurface with flour. Pinch off a small piece of the dough, gently roll it on the worksurface, using the tines of a fork, and dust with flour. Place on a floured pan or cutting board. Repeat until all the dough is used up, to make approximately 45 gnocchis.

5 Bring a large pan of water to a boil. Cook the gnocchi in small batches for approximately 2 to 3 minutes—they'll be ready when they float to the top of the water. Remove with a slotted spoon and keep warm in a loosely covered bowl while you cook the rest. Serve with Two-Step Tomato Sauce or Pistachio, Parsley, and Walnut Pesto.

PEARL BARLEY
RISOTTO
with glazed balsamic root vegetables

serves 4

Pearl barley is really underused in my opinion and makes a great alternative to rice in risotto-style dishes. It takes a little longer to cook, but it's so worth the wait, as it really absorbs the flavors in the pan and makes for what can only be described as an unctuous plate of awesomeness. The balsamic roasted root vegetables are the perfect yin to the yang of the creamy risotto, and even though I like to use things like soy cream sparingly (if at all), I'm happy to make an exception here.

INGREDIENTS

For the risotto
1 vegetable bouillon cube
1 tablespoon olive oil
2 leeks, finely chopped
salt and freshly ground
black pepper
1 cup pearl barley
½ cup soy cream
1 tablespoon Dijon mustard

For the vegetables
2 carrots, cubed
1 parsnip, cubed
1 beet, cubed
½ butternut squash, cubed
1 garlic clove, crushed
2 tablespoons balsamic vinegar
4 teaspoons extra virgin olive oil
1 tablespoon agave nectar
2 sprigs thyme
extra virgin olive oil and thyme
leaves, to garnish

METHOD

1 Preheat the oven to 400°F. Bring 1 quart water to a boil in a large saucepan, crumble in the vegetable bouillon cube, and reduce the heat to very low.

2 Heat the olive oil in a large, heavy-bottomed pan. Add the leeks, season with salt and pepper, and allow to soften slowly, ensuring they don't brown.

3 Place the cubed root vegetables in a heatproof dish. Whisk the garlic, vinegar, oil, and agave nectar together in a small bowl. Pour into the vegetables, ensuring everything is thoroughly coated, season with salt and pepper, and tuck in the thyme sprigs. Roast the vegetables in the oven for 40 minutes, stirring occasionally.

4 Add the pearl barley to the pan with the leeks, allowing it to soak up some of the excess oil before adding 2 to 3 ladles of hot stock. Cook the barley fairly rapidly until the stock is absorbed. Repeat, adding a few ladlefuls of stock at a time, until almost all the stock has been used. This will take at least an hour. Toward the end of the cooking time, pour in the soy cream and mustard, stir well, and season to taste.

5 To serve, divide the risotto between four shallow bowls and make a well in the center. Spoon in one-quarter of the glazed vegetables and finish with a splash of olive oil and some fresh thyme leaves.

PEA AND LEMON
RISOTTO
with a mint oil drizzle

serves 2 to 4

Risotto is a mainstay in my kitchen. Call me weird, but I actually like having to stand by the stove for 20 minutes… all that stirring is downright therapeutic. It shows in the eating too, as every minute of that effort renders a perfectly *al dente* rice dish, which doesn't feel remotely lacking despite the cheese omission. The mint oil drizzle is so rich and flavorful, I truly believe that even adding vegan Parmesan would be a crime. You also want the lemon to really sing here, and adding anything extra would simply dull that fresh and zesty taste. This is risotto stripped right back and, truth be told, it's all the better for it.

INGREDIENTS

For the mint oil
¾ cup mint leaves, finely chopped
2 tablespoons extra virgin olive oil
salt and freshly ground
black pepper

For the risotto
1 vegetable bouillon cube
2 tablespoons olive oil
1 onion, finely chopped
3 garlic cloves, finely chopped
1 cup arborio rice
1½ cups frozen peas
5½oz baby spinach
grated zest and juice of 1 lemon

METHOD

1 Begin by making the mint oil, as it will need time to infuse fully. Place the mint leaves in a small bowl, add the olive oil, season with salt and pepper, and stir vigorously. Set aside to infuse at room temperature until needed.

2 Bring 1 quart water to a boil in a large saucepan, add the crumbled bouillon cube, then reduce the heat to very low.

3 Heat the oil in a large pan, add the onion, season, and allow to soften for several minutes. Add the garlic to the pan and cook for a few minutes, ensuring it doesn't brown.

4 Add the rice and stir well for a minute or two to allow the grains to absorb the flavors. Ladle in enough hot stock to just cover the rice, then simmer over medium heat for several minutes, stirring constantly until the grains have absorbed all of the liquid. Add the remaining stock, a ladleful at a time, stirring constantly, until each ladleful is absorbed and the rice is cooked through. This will take around 20 to 25 minutes.

5 Defrost the peas by covering them with freshly boiled water, leave for 5 minutes, and then drain. Add to the pan along with the spinach and lemon juice. Stir until the spinach is wilted. Taste, season again if necessary, and serve garnished with the lemon zest and drizzled with the mint oil.

~tortilla~ PIZZAS

serves 2 as a main course or 4 as an appetizer

Sometimes it's nice to skip the time-consuming part and get straight to it. This is where the unsuspecting tortilla comes into play, allowing us a little taste of Italy with none of the usual "knead, rest, bake" shenanigans. I've found that hummus makes a great cheese alternative here and also adds a great flavor hit. The other toppings are just a suggestion, but you could throw just about anything on if you wish. Just remember not to pile the fillings too high, or you might have a very messy meal in store!

INGREDIENTS

3½oz spinach
½ cup hummus
juice of ½ lemon
freshly ground black pepper
¼ cup tomato paste
½ teaspoon garlic purée
4 large flour tortillas
½ red onion, finely sliced
4 artichoke hearts (from a jar), chopped
½ cup pitted black olives, sliced
2 tablespoons capers in brine, drained and rinsed
flour, for dusting

METHOD

1 Preheat the oven to 425°F. Place an upside down baking sheet in the oven to preheat—this will be the "pizza stone."

2 Bring a small pan of water to a boil. Blanch the spinach for a few minutes, drain, squeeze out any excess liquid, and then chop into a pulp. Set aside.

3 Combine the hummus and lemon juice thoroughly in a bowl to form a pourable sauce. Season with black pepper and set aside.

4 Combine the tomato paste with the garlic purée and a splash of water to thin out the resulting sauce. Stack 2 tortillas for each pizza—doubling them creates a firm base for the topping. Spread the sauce over the bases, leaving a gap around the edge of each pizza.

5 Now layer the topping, starting with the spinach, followed by the red onion, artichokes, olives, and finally the capers. Generously drizzle with the hummus sauce.

6 Flour the preheated baking sheet (still upside down). Carefully transfer the pizza to the sheet using a large spatula. Bake for 8 to 10 minutes, checking it occasionally. Cut into quarters and serve. If you bake both pizzas at the same time on separate shelves, the top one may take slightly longer to cook.

~ thick-crust ~
MUSHROOM PIZZA

serves 2 to 3

This pizza recipe has a homemade crust—still with a bit of a short-cut, though! I always try to make recipes easier and I predict this will soon come in very handy when I have children's mealtimes to juggle. As before, we're keeping prep time to an absolute minimum (although a little kneading is required), which means we can get this pizza on the table in less than 30 minutes—sound good? Let's go.

INGREDIENTS

For the pizza dough
2 cups bread flour, plus extra
for dusting
pinch of sugar
$1/2$ teaspoon salt
$1/2$ teaspoon baking powder
$1/2$ teaspoon active dry yeast
$1/2$ cup soy milk or water
2 tablespoons olive oil, plus extra
for greasing

For the cashew cheese
1 cup cashews, soaked in cold
water for at least 6 hours
juice of $1/2$ lemon
$1/2$ teaspoon salt
$1/2$ teaspoon Dijon mustard

For the topping
3 to 4 tablespoons tomato sauce
2 tablespoons Tapenade (page 135)
2 cups mixed mushrooms, sliced
1 tablespoon dried oregano
or thyme

METHOD

1 To make the dough, mix the flour, sugar, salt, baking powder, and yeast together in a large bowl. Combine the milk or water and oil in a bowl.

2 Make a well in the center of the flour mixture and pour in half of the liquid. Using your hands, work the flour into the liquid in a clockwise motion, adding more liquid when needed. Once the mixture forms a ball of dough, turn it onto a lightly floured worksurface and knead for several minutes until the dough is smooth and elastic.

3 Place the dough in an oiled bowl, cover with a kitchen towel, and set aside for 10 minutes.

4 Preheat the oven to 475°F. Place an upside down baking sheet in the oven to preheat—this will be the "pizza stone."

5 Drain the cashews and place in a blender. Add $1/2$ cup water, the lemon juice, and salt. Blend until smooth, adding more water if necessary. Add the Dijon mustard and blend again until well combined. Season and set aside.

6 Roll out the dough to form one large pizza base or divide in half to make two smaller ones and transfer to a cutting board. Spread the pizza dough with the sauce and top with the tapenade, sliced mushrooms, and oregano or thyme leaves. Spoon over the cashew cheese and spread it out. Carefully transfer to the heated baking sheet. Bake for 10 to 15 minutes or until the crust is crispy.

SANTORINI-STYLE
SPAGHETTI
with lemon, capers, and tomatoes

serves 4

Santorini is such a glorious holiday destination—I've never been so blown away by such a charming little island, and I honestly cannot wait to go back. With all its wonderful fresh produce, including glorious tomatoes, magnificent capers, and preservative-free wine (*sayonara* hangovers!) it really is a foodie haven, and one that I have desperately tried to recreate in my own kitchen. If you're worried about what it's like to travel and still stay vegan, Santorini is seriously the place for you—even the delicious frothy coffee doesn't contain milk and the people could not be more accommodating. This spaghetti dish is a slight variation on one I sampled in the main town of Fira, and it really was a highlight of our last trip there… and, yes, I actually do have food on the brain, but with wholesome food like this, who can blame me?

INGREDIENTS

2 tablespoons olive oil
3 shallots, finely sliced
salt and freshly ground
black pepper
3 garlic cloves, finely chopped
1¾ cups cherry or other small
tomatoes, halved
14oz spaghetti
juice of 1 lemon
2 tablespoons capers in
brine, drained, rinsed, and
roughly chopped
½ cup medium vegan white wine
1 tablespoon extra virgin olive oil
freshly chopped flat-leaf parsley,
to garnish

METHOD

1 Bring a large pan of salted water to a boil.

2 Heat the olive oil in a large, non-stick, heavy-bottomed frying pan and add the shallots. Season with salt and pepper and allow the shallots to sweat for several minutes before adding the garlic and tomatoes.

3 Add the pasta to the pan of boiling water and cook according to the package instructions, stirring frequently to keep it from sticking.

4 Once the tomatoes begin to soften, pour in the lemon juice, season, and reduce for a few minutes. Add the capers and wine to the pan—turn the heat up and let the alcohol evaporate and the sauce thicken slightly.

5 Reserve a small cup of cooking water from the pasta before draining it. Lightly toss the spaghetti in the sauce. Pour in the reserved cooking water and let the pasta soak up the sauce flavors before transferring to a dish.

6 Serve drizzled with the extra virgin olive oil and a sprinkling of freshly chopped parsley.

MACARO-NO CHEESE
with crispy kale

serves 2 to 4

The one thing I often encounter when people discover I'm vegan is an immediate lamentation for my cheese-less existence. It's true that cheese is no longer a part of my life, and despite having previously spent most of my days as a total dairy fiend, even I can't quite fathom why I simply don't miss it. Perhaps in part it has a lot to do with dishes like this one, which perfectly replicates that ultimate comfort food feel—and something tells me you won't be boo-hooing about the lack of Cheddar either.

INGREDIENTS

1 × 1¾lb butternut squash, halved
and seeded
¾ cup coconut milk
1 scant teaspoon Dijon mustard
½ vegetable bouillon cube
1 teaspoon cider vinegar
salt and freshly ground
black pepper
9oz macaroni

For the crispy kale
1 tablespoon olive oil
2¼ cups kale, torn into
bite-sized pieces
1 teaspoon sea salt flakes

METHOD

1 Preheat the oven to 400°F.

2 Place the squash, flesh side down, in a roasting pan and pour in about ½ cup water. Bake in the oven for 1 hour or until the flesh is completely soft. Leave the oven at the same temperature to cook the kale later on. Set the squash aside to cool slightly before scooping out the flesh with a spoon and blending with the coconut milk to a smooth purée in a blender.

3 Pour the purée into a saucepan and bring to a gentle simmer before adding the Dijon mustard, crumbled bouillon cube, and cider vinegar. Season with salt and pepper and add a little water to loosen the sauce. Continue to simmer for another 20 minutes until it thickens and turns pale yellow.

4 Bring a large pan of salted water to boil. Add the pasta and cook for just slightly under the recommended time.

5 While the pasta is cooking, rub the olive oil all over the kale pieces. Spread out on a baking sheet and bake in the oven for 8 to 10 minutes or until completely crisp. Sprinkle sea salt flakes over the top.

5 Drain the macaroni and transfer to the pan of squash sauce. Stir to combine and heat through gently over low heat for about 5 minutes. Serve in heated bowls and top with the salty, crispy kale.

SIMPLE HERB PASTA
with slow—roasted tomatoes

serves 4

This super green pasta dish definitely hits the spot. It's a miracle I actually had the patience to wait for these slow-roasted tomatoes, but they really add something special to this dish—even though 8 hours might feel like an ungodly time to wait for some people. Served hot or cold, it's packed full of fresh flavors, with those tomatoes just about stealing the show… so omit them at your peril!

INGREDIENTS

For the tomatoes
5 large tomatoes, halved
1 tablespoon balsamic vinegar
2 tablespoons olive oil
salt and freshly ground
black pepper
1 tablespoon dried herbes
de Provence

For the pasta
¾ cup each of fresh flat-leaf
parsley, cilantro, and basil
¼ fennel bulb, roughly chopped
1 celery rib, roughly chopped
½ onion, roughly chopped
2 garlic cloves
juice of 1 lemon
2 tablespoons olive oil
9oz mini pasta shapes,
such as conchigliette
1 vegetable bouillon cube
Greek basil and olive oil, to serve

METHOD

1 Preheat the oven to 225°F.

2 Place the tomatoes in a roasting pan and cover evenly with the balsamic, 1 tablespoon of the oil, 1 teaspoon salt, ½ teaspoon black pepper, and the herbes de Provence. Roast for 7 to 8 hours and set aside to cool. Before serving, drizzle with the remaining oil.

3 For the pasta, put the herbs, fennel, celery, onion, garlic, lemon juice, and olive oil into a food processor with some salt and pepper and blend until they form a coarse paste. Transfer the paste to a large, non-stick, heavy-bottomed frying pan and cook it gently for 5 to 7 minutes. Add the pasta shapes to the pan and stir well to coat in the paste. Sprinkle over the crumbled bouillon cube and cover the pasta completely with cold water. Bring to a boil and then simmer gently until all the water is absorbed, adding a little more if necessary, until the pasta is fully cooked, stirring frequently.

4 Eat hot or allow to cool to room temperature and serve with the tomatoes, scattered with the Greek basil and a drizzle of olive oil.

SOMETHING
Special

BLOODY MARY BRUSCHETTA

BELL PEPPER AND PEA PARTY
FRITTATAS

BALSAMIC AND BLACK PEPPERCORN
CASHEW CHEESE

ASPARAGUS, MINTED PEA, AND
CARAMELIZED RED ONION TART

BAKED EGGPLANT WITH
LEMON-INFUSED COUSCOUS

SMOKY MOROCCAN CHICKPEA STEW
WITH SAFFRON-INFUSED COUSCOUS

SWEDISH-STYLE VEGBALLS
WITH MASHED POTATOES AND
MUSTARD SAUCE

SHEPHERDESS PIE WITH
SWEET POTATO TOPPING

MEXICAN-STYLE LASAGNA

RED LENTIL AND SPINACH LASAGNA

INDIAN-SPICED TACOS WITH
MANGO SALSA

SUMMERTIME STEW

BEET, CITRUS, AND
FENNEL SALAD

ZESTY BULGUR WHEAT AND
WATERMELON SALAD

SWEET POTATO AND SPINACH SUSHI

STRAWBERRY MARGARITA

CHERRY GINGER FIZZ

HITCHCOCK BLONDE COCKTAIL

bloody mary BRUSCHETTA

serves 8 to 12

Who said alcohol should be confined to drinks? I often add a little whisky to cream sauce or tequila to homemade salsa, so why not vodka on bruschetta? A terrific appetizer for brunch or dinner, these little morsels of booze-infused naughtiness will soon get you on the road to recovery (if it's the hair of the dog you're seeking) or kick-start your evening with a bang. Now that's music to my Bloody Mary-lovin' ears.

INGREDIENTS

1 small baguette
1 garlic clove
3 to 4 tablespoons extra virgin olive oil
4 large ripe tomatoes (at room temperature), roughly chopped
1 tablespoon lemon juice
2 tablespoons vodka
1 teaspoon balsamic vinegar
¼ teaspoon Tabasco sauce
salt and freshly ground black pepper
1 celery rib with leaves

METHOD

1 Preheat a grill pan over medium heat or preheat the broiler. Cut the baguette into about 15 medium slices. Rub each piece with the garlic clove, drizzle with a little extra virgin olive oil, and very lightly toast both sides of the slices on the grill pan or under the broiler.

2 Place the chopped tomatoes in a bowl along with the lemon juice, vodka, balsamic vinegar, and Tabasco. Season with salt and pepper and stir well to combine.

3 Take the leaves off the celery rib and reserve for later. Finely dice the celery and add to the tomato mixture. Season to taste and then divide the mixture evenly between the baguette toasts.

4 Roughly chop the reserved celery leaves and sprinkle over the bruschetta with a final drizzle of extra virgin olive oil and a little extra freshly ground black pepper. Serve immediately.

TIP
You could also top the bruschetta with chopped black olives.

bell pepper and pea party FRITTATAS

serves 6 to 8

Party food ideas can sometimes be challenging when catering for vegans, and I never expect anything more than dip and crudités when I'm invited over to someone else's house. To avoid any embarrassment (for them and me), I whip up a batch of these to take with me and they always go down ridiculously well... sometimes a bit too well—"Ahem, leave some for me!"

INGREDIENTS

1 tablespoon sunflower oil
1 onion, finely chopped
salt and freshly ground
black pepper
1 red bell pepper, seeded and
chopped into small dice
2 large garlic cloves,
finely chopped
1¼ cups frozen peas
¾ cup fresh flat-leaf parsley,
chopped
14oz firm tofu
1 teaspoon ground turmeric
1 tablespoon cornstarch
¼ teaspoon Dijon mustard
¼ to ½ cup soy milk

METHOD

1 Preheat the oven to 400˚F.

2 Heat the oil in a large frying pan. Add the onion to the pan, season with salt and pepper, and cook for several minutes, ensuring the onion doesn't brown.

3 Add the red bell pepper to the pan and cook gently until softened. Add the garlic and peas, plus 1 tablespoon water. Season and cook for a few minutes until the peas are defrosted. Stir in the chopped parsley. Set aside.

4 Drain the tofu and press out any excess water—place it in a shallow bowl, rest a plate on top of the tofu, and place 2 × 14oz food cans on the plate. Set aside for 20 minutes, then pat dry with a clean kitchen towel.

5 Break the tofu into pieces and place in a food processor along with the turmeric, cornstarch, Dijon mustard, ¼ cup soy milk, and a generous dose of salt and pepper. Process until smooth, adding more soy milk only if the mixture is too thick—the consistency should be like soft whipped cream.

6 Pour the mixture into a large bowl and stir in the onion, bell pepper, and pea mixture until it is fully combined.

7 Spoon the mixture into 8 standard-sized silicon muffin cups, filling each one to the top, and bake for 30 minutes. Let cool and then chill in their cups until required—they'll keep for several days. Serve cold.

balsamic and black peppercorn
CASHEW CHEESE

serves 4 to 6

When I first embraced this lifestyle I hadn't the faintest clue about vegan cheeses. In fact, the first processed "cheese" I tasted was pretty vile, so it was a long time before I was willing to subject my taste buds to it again. You can imagine how floored I was, then, when I came across the first utterance of a thing called "cashew cheese"—it piqued my curiosity so much, I had to do some recipe delving myself, and I was definitely not disappointed. Over the years (and with the help of my husband as chief taste-tester), I've developed several easy cashew cheeses. This one looks particularly impressive on a cheeseboard, flanked by grapes and crackers—and my friends are still bamboozled when I tell them it's made from nuts. With cashews as the base, you can add just about anything you want to, but I adore the balance between the sweet, tangy balsamic vinegar and aromatic black peppercorns—plus, you get a wickedly crunchy exterior. Serve with crackers and the obligatory glass of red wine for the perfect finale to your undoubtedly impressive vegan soirée.

INGREDIENTS

1 cup cashews

3 tablespoons balsamic vinegar

1 tablespoon dried mixed herbs

2 to 3 teaspoons coarse sea salt

1 tablespoon cracked black pepper, plus extra for rolling

METHOD

1 Soak the cashews in water overnight.

2 Drain and rinse the cashews and place them in a food processor along with the balsamic vinegar, herbs, and salt and pepper. Process until smooth, scraping down the sides with a spatula occasionally. It will take around 10 to 15 minutes before you achieve the desired consistency, which is similar to that of a soft goat cheese or a spreadable cheese such as Boursin. You may need to add 1/2 to 1 tablespoon of water, but be careful not to add too much.

3 Line a cutting board with plastic wrap. Transfer the cashew mixture to the board and use the plastic wrap to shape it into a log. Wrap tightly and place in the freezer for 1 hour to firm.

4 Remove from the freezer and keep in the fridge until needed. Just before serving, roll the cheese in cracked black peppercorns for a final flourish.

asparagus, minted pea, and caramelized
RED ONION TART

serves 4

I'm not shy about using the occasional store-bought ingredient, and reaching for ready-made puff pastry is one of the few concessions I allow when it comes to making a quick 'n' easy tart. Call it a short cut (or sheer laziness) but this is one of the easiest ways I know to get dinner on the table without too much fuss. The caramelized red onions require a little patience; however, the result is a delicious trio of flavors that will more than make up for your pastry-making skills… or lack thereof, as the case may be.

INGREDIENTS

For the caramelized onions
3 tablespoons olive oil
4 red onions, finely sliced
salt and freshly ground black pepper
1 teaspoon dried thyme
1 tablespoon sugar
dash of red wine vinegar

For the pea purée
3¼ cups frozen peas
¾ cup fresh mint leaves, roughly
chopped, plus extra to garnish
2 tablespoons olive oil
juice of 1 lemon

one 13½ × 8½in sheet
rolled puff pastry
10½oz asparagus spears,
halved lengthwise
olive oil, to drizzle
grated zest of 1 lemon
coarse sea salt

METHOD

1 For the onions, heat 2 tablespoons of the oil in a medium, non-stick, heavy-bottomed frying pan. Add the onions and season with salt and pepper. Cook for several minutes before sprinkling with the dried thyme and sugar. Once the onions begin to soften, add a dash of red wine vinegar. Add the remaining oil if necessary and let cook gently for 30 minutes until completely soft.

2 Meanwhile, to make the pea purée, place the peas in a bowl, cover with freshly boiled water, and let sit for a few minutes. Drain the peas and place in a food processor along with the chopped mint, olive oil, and lemon juice. Season and process to form a coarse purée. Set aside.

3 Preheat the oven to 400°F. Cut the pastry sheet into 4 equal rectangles and place on 2 baking sheets.

4 Leaving about a ½in border around the edge of each pastry rectangle, spread a quarter of the pea purée over each square followed by a quarter of the caramelized onions. Arrange the halved asparagus spears over the onions—you should be able to fit 5 halves on each tart. Drizzle with a little olive oil, season, and bake in the oven for 25 to 30 minutes.

5 Finish with the lemon zest, a fine sprinkling of freshly chopped mint, and a pinch of coarse sea salt. Serve warm. These tarts are delicious served alongside an arugula and avocado salad.

BAKED EGGPLANT
with lemon-infused couscous

serves 2

I love couscous an inordinate amount. Often mistaken for a grain, it's actually more akin to pasta as it is made from tiny granules of durum wheat. While you could use a protein-packed option like quinoa (and feel free to do so), there's something so tempting about a mouthful of lemon-infused couscous.

INGREDIENTS

1 eggplant, halved lengthwise
2 teaspoons harissa
4 to 5 tablespoons olive oil
salt and freshly ground
black pepper
3/4 cup couscous
pared strips of zest from 1/2 lemon
juice of 1 lemon
1 teaspoon smoked paprika
3 tablespoons pine nuts, toasted
3/4 cup fresh flat-leaf parsley,
chopped, plus extra to garnish
1 teaspoon sesame seeds, toasted,
to garnish

For the tahini dressing
1/2 cup tahini
2 tablespoons lemon juice
2 tablespoons olive oil
1 tablespoon maple syrup or
agave nectar
1/4 teaspoon salt

METHOD

1 Preheat the oven to 350°F and lightly oil a baking sheet.

2 Score the eggplant flesh diagonally both ways, creating a diamond pattern. Place on the baking sheet. Spread a teaspoon of harissa over each half, covering all the crevices. Drizzle 1 tablespoon of the oil over each, season with salt and pepper, and bake for 40 minutes or until the flesh is completely soft, turning over halfway through to ensure the skin doesn't crisp or dry out.

3 Place the couscous in a bowl with the lemon zest strips. Add 2/3 cup freshly boiled water, cover, and set aside until all the liquid has been absorbed—about 10 minutes. Discard the lemon zest and fluff the couscous with a fork.

4 Scoop the flesh from the center of each eggplant half, leaving enough around the sides to keep its shape. Roughly chop the flesh and place in a bowl. Stir through the couscous along with the lemon juice, smoked paprika, and remaining olive oil. Season, then add the toasted pine nuts and parsley. Divide the mixture evenly between the eggplant skins. Return to the baking sheet and bake for another 15 to 20 minutes.

5 To make the dressing, place the tahini in a bowl with the lemon juice, oil, maple syrup or agave nectar, salt, and 2 tablespoons water. Whisk until smooth, adding a little more water if necessary—or use a hand-held blender.

6 Remove the stuffed eggplants from the oven and serve with a dollop of tahini dressing and a sprinkling of sesame seeds and parsley.

SMOKY MOROCCAN CHICKPEA STEW

with saffron-infused couscous

serves 2 to 4

Smoky, sweet, sticky, and savory stew. That's probably what I should have called this dish, but its obtuseness might have got in the way of its greatness—and I wouldn't want there to be any confusion in the matter because this dish is the epitome of deliciousness.

INGREDIENTS

2 tablespoons sunflower oil
1 red onion, roughly chopped
1 red bell pepper, seeded and
roughly chopped
1 carrot, roughly chopped
salt and freshly ground
black pepper
2 garlic cloves, finely chopped
1 eggplant, cubed
4 large tomatoes
1 teaspoon ground cumin
1 teaspoon smoked paprika
½ teaspoon ground coriander
½ teaspoon ground cinnamon
1 tablespoon tomato paste
1 × 14oz can chickpeas
5 medjool dates
1½ cups couscous
pinch of saffron strands
pared zest and juice of 1 lemon
1 teaspoon vegetable stock granules
3 tablespoons extra virgin olive oil
¾ cup fresh flat-leaf parsley,
chopped

METHOD

1 Heat half the oil in a medium, heavy-bottomed saucepan. Add the onion, red bell pepper, and carrot, season with salt and pepper, and sauté for several minutes before stirring in the garlic. Add the eggplant to the pan with the remaining oil, cover, and let the vegetables soften for 5 to 10 minutes, stirring every so often.

2 Place the whole tomatoes in a medium bowl, cover with boiling water, and set aside for 1 minute. Remove the skins from the tomatoes and finely chop the flesh.

3 Sprinkle the spices over the cooking vegetables, allowing the flavors to infuse for several minutes, before adding the chopped tomatoes. Season and bring to a gentle simmer.

4 When the tomatoes have broken up a little and are beginning to look more sauce-like, add the tomato paste. Stir to combine, season, cover, and simmer until the vegetables are soft—around 20 minutes. Finally, drain and rinse the chickpeas, and pit and chop the dates. Add the chickpeas and dates to the pan and cook gently for another 10 minutes.

5 Meanwhile, place the couscous in a bowl with the saffron strands and the lemon zest strips. Dissolve the vegetable stock granules in 1 cup boiling water and pour over the couscous. Cover and let sit for 5 to 10 minutes until all the water has been absorbed. Remove the lemon zest and fluff with a fork. Add the lemon juice, extra virgin olive oil, and flat-leaf parsley and stir. Divide the couscous between plates and serve topped with the stew.

SWEDISH-STYLE VEGBALLS
with mashed potatoes and mustard sauce

serves 2 to 3

I'm always a bit loathe to describe anything vegan as being "meaty," which is why I've gone with the "vegball" title here. Instead of the typical dill sauce served with these traditional Scandavian-style "meat" balls (and, yes, I'm kinda referring to the sort served at a certain Swedish homestore) I've gone for a more robust mustard accompaniment, which I think works really well alongside the earthy lentils. The polenta coating gives the balls a wonderfully crunchy exterior that should satisfy every guest at your table.

INGREDIENTS

1 × 14oz can green lentils, drained and rinsed
½ teaspoon garlic powder
or 1 large garlic clove, very finely chopped
3 tablespoons all-purpose flour
½ cup polenta
sunflower oil, for shallow-frying
salt and freshly ground black pepper

For the mashed potatoes
4 potatoes, chopped into small chunks
1 tablespoon vegan margarine

For the creamy mustard sauce
14oz coconut milk
1 teaspoon cider vinegar
1 tablespoon cornstarch
1 heaping tablespoon whole-grain mustard

METHOD

1 Place the lentils in a bowl with the garlic powder or chopped garlic and 1 tablespoon of the flour. Season and stir well. Refrigerate for 30 minutes.

2 Pour the polenta and the remaining flour into separate shallow bowls. Divide the lentil mixture into 10 equal portions and roll each portion into a ball. Coat each ball in flour and then in polenta (reserve the leftover polenta for a second coating before cooking). Place on a baking sheet lined with parchment paper and chill for 30 minutes maximum.

3 Bring a medium pan of salted water to a boil, add the potato chunks, and simmer for 15 to 20 minutes or until the potatoes are soft. Drain and mash with the vegan margarine. Season, cover, and set aside.

4 Place the coconut milk and cider vinegar in a shallow frying pan, season, and bring to a gentle simmer. Mix the cornstarch with a little coconut milk in a cup before pouring it into the sauce. Stir constantly and, when the sauce has thickened, stir in the whole-grain mustard and heat through. Taste for seasoning. Keep warm over very low heat, stirring occasionally.

5 Pour about ¾in of sunflower oil into a medium, shallow, non-stick frying pan. Heat the oil until hot but not smoking. Roll the vegballs in the remaining polenta and gently fry in batches of 3 to 4 until golden and crispy all over. Keep warm in a low oven 300°F while you cook the remainder. Serve the vegballs with the mash and creamy mustard sauce.

SHEPHERDESS PIE

with sweet potato topping

serves 4

Being Irish, I have a major penchant for the humble spud, but feel I should at least try to break away from my potato-loving roots now and then, and give some other equally wonderful vegetables a fighting chance. Besides, the sweet potato is a brilliant match to the rich tomato sauce in this pie, especially when paired with the distinctive dill addition, which really brings this whole plate alive.

INGREDIENTS

1 tablespoon olive oil
1 small leek, finely chopped
1 parsnip, diced
1 carrot, diced
1 celery rib, sliced
1 tablespoon herbes de Provence
salt and freshly ground
black pepper
2 garlic cloves, finely chopped
2 tablespoons balsamic vinegar
1 × 14oz can chopped tomatoes
1 tablespoon tomato paste
1 teaspoon Marmite
1 teaspoon sugar
1 × 14oz can green lentils
1 cup frozen peas

For the mashed sweet potato
4 sweet potatoes, chopped into
small chunks
1 teaspoon vegan margarine
1 heaping teaspoon Dijon mustard
½ cup dill, roughly chopped

METHOD

1 Heat the oil in a large frying pan and add the leek, parsnip, carrot, celery, and herbs. Season with salt and pepper and gently sauté until the vegetables begin to soften.

2 Add the garlic and half the balsamic vinegar. Season again and cook for 10 minutes before adding the chopped tomatoes, tomato paste, and ½ cup water. Season and add the remaining balsamic vinegar, the Marmite, sugar, and a splash of water. Simmer for 20 minutes, adding a little more water now and then to loosen the sauce and crushing the tomatoes further with the back of a spoon.

3 For the mashed sweet potato, bring a large pan of salted water to a boil, add the potato chunks, and simmer for 15 to 20 minutes or until the potatoes are soft. Drain and mash with the vegan margarine. Season and stir in the mustard and dill and return to low heat. Keep stirring until the potatoes are dry and firm—around 5 minutes. Take off the heat and set aside.

4 Preheat the oven to 350°F. Drain and rinse the lentils, then add to the tomato sauce. Add the frozen peas to the sauce and cook for another 5 minutes before transferring to an 8in baking dish. Spoon the mash on top, ensuring the lentil mixture is completely covered in potato.

5 Bake in the oven for 25 to 30 minutes or until bubbling. Remove from the oven and let cool for 5 to 10 minutes before serving.

mexican-style LASAGNA

serves 4

When you think of lasagna, do you automatically envisage slaving over a white sauce and praying that the pasta will cook through? If, like me, you enjoy the idea of diving into layers of delicious filling but can't always be bothered with the hassle, this Mexican lasagna could be the perfect halfway house that will go some way toward satisfying those all-too-frequent comfort-food needs. The inside may not exactly resemble the traditional Italian version but I doubt you'll care once you realize it tastes just as good… if not a little better.

INGREDIENTS

For the refried beans
1 tablespoon sunflower oil
1 onion, finely chopped
salt and freshly ground
black pepper
2 garlic cloves, finely chopped
1 heaping teaspoon ground cumin
1 teaspoon paprika
1 × 14oz can borlotti or pinto beans, drained and rinsed
few sprigs thyme, leaves removed and roughly chopped
1 vegetable bouillon cube
2 bay leaves

For the tomato sauce
1 tablespoon sunflower oil
1 red chile, seeded and finely chopped
2 garlic cloves, finely chopped

METHOD

1 For the refried beans, heat the oil in a medium saucepan and add the onion. Season with salt and pepper and allow the onion to soften gently for several minutes. Add the garlic along with the cumin and paprika. Cook for a few more minutes.

2 Add the borlotti beans and thyme leaves to the pan. Season, cover with water, add the bouillon cube and bay leaves, and simmer for 30 to 40 minutes, adding more water if necessary.

3 Remove the bay leaves and mash the beans using the back of a fork or a masher. Keep warm over very low heat, stirring frequently. If the sauce becomes too dry, just add a little more water to loosen it.

4 For the tomato sauce, heat the oil in a pan and lightly cook the chile and garlic, ensuring the garlic does not brown.

5 Add the tomatoes along with the tomato paste, sugar, spices and 1 tablespoon water. Season, then crush the tomatoes with the back of a spoon and allow to gently simmer for 30 minutes, adding another 1 to 2 tablespoons water, if necessary, to prevent the sauce from becoming too thick.

6 For the roasted sweet potatoes, preheat the oven to 300°F.

mexican–style LASAGNA continued...

INGREDIENTS

1 × 14oz can chopped tomatoes
1 tablespoon tomato paste
pinch of sugar
¼ teaspoon cayenne pepper
½ teaspoon paprika

For the roasted sweet potatoes
2 large sweet potatoes, scrubbed
and cut into large chunks
1 teaspoon smoked paprika
1 tablespoon olive oil

For the other layers
4 flour tortillas
1¾ cups frozen sweet corn,
thawed in warm water and drained
1 × 14oz can black beans, drained
and rinsed
chopped cilantro, to garnish

METHOD

7 Place the potato chunks on a baking sheet, sprinkle in the paprika and drizzle with the oil, season well, and toss to coat. Roast in the oven for 30 to 40 minutes. Remove from the oven and set aside, but leave the oven on at the same temperature to bake the lasagna.

8 To assemble the lasagna, coat the bottom of an 8in baking dish with a small amount of tomato sauce—just enough so the tortillas don't stick to the bottom. Halve all the tortillas and arrange them all over the sauce, so the straight edges meet the sides of the dish.

9 Spread half of the refried beans onto the tortillas, spoon over half the sweet corn and black beans, and top with half the roasted sweet potatoes and a little tomato sauce.

10 Repeat the layers with the remaining refried beans, sweet corn, black beans, and potatoes. Top with most of the remaining tomato sauce, reserving a little for serving later.

11 Bake the lasagna in the oven for 30 minutes.

12 Thin out the reserved tomato sauce with a splash of water and heat it through. Pour over the lasagna and garnish with chopped cilantro, to serve.

red lentil and
SPINACH LASAGNA

serves 4 to 6

I've always been a huge fan of lasagna and this fantastic meat-free version isn't too much of a headache to construct… even on a wearisome weekday evening. There aren't any tomatoes in the sauce or cheese on top, but the flavors contained within will have you sidling back for more—or I'll eat my hat. The spinach base is a nice surprise that you could easily substitute with kale or any other leafy green. And do use freshly grated nutmeg rather than ground, or your béchamel will end up tasting more like a latte than a savory sauce.

INGREDIENTS

For the lentil layers
1 tablespoon oil
1 onion, finely diced
1 carrot, finely diced
1 parsnip, finely diced
salt and freshly ground
black pepper
1 sprig rosemary, leaves finely
chopped
1¼ cup red lentils
1 vegetable bouillon cube

For the pasta and spinach layers
7oz spinach
1 tablespoon olive oil
9 lasagna sheets
freshly grated nutmeg, to season

METHOD

1 For the lentil layers, heat the oil in a medium, heavy-bottomed saucepan. Add the vegetables, season with salt and pepper, and cook gently until they begin to soften. Add the rosemary and cook for another 5 minutes.

2 Add the lentils, stir to combine, and cover with cold water. Crumble the bouillon cube into the pan, bring to a gentle simmer, and stir frequently to prevent the lentils from sticking. Once most of the liquid has been absorbed, add more water until the lentils are cooked; they should be soft but not mushy—this should take around 15 to 20 minutes. Set aside.

3 Preheat the oven to 350°F. Bring a large pan of water to a boil and blanch the spinach for several minutes until it is just wilted. Remove with a slotted spoon and press firmly to release any excess water.

4 In the same pan, add the olive oil before dropping in the lasagna sheets. Cook the sheets until they are *al dente*, but be careful not to overcook. Drain, rinse with cold water, and set aside until needed.

5 For the sauce, melt the butter in a pan and add the flour, stirring until it thickens. Add half the soy milk, stirring constantly until smooth. Season, add the nutmeg, mustard, vinegar, and remaining milk. Cook until smooth and glossy, stirring occasionally—add a little more milk or water if it becomes too thick. Check the seasoning and then assemble the lasagna.

INGREDIENTS

For the béchamel sauce
2 tablespoons vegan butter
4 tablespoons flour
1¼ cups soy milk
1 teaspoon freshly grated nutmeg
1 teaspoon Dijon mustard
1 teaspoon cider vinegar

METHOD

6 Arrange the spinach in the bottom of a lightly greased 8in baking dish. Season with pepper and nutmeg and pour in one-third of the béchamel sauce. Place three lasagna sheets on top, then half the lentil mixture, another three lasagna sheets, the remaining lentils, and finally the last sheets of pasta. Pour in the rest of the béchamel and a generous grating of nutmeg.

7 Bake for 20 to 25 minutes until the top begins to bubble and turns golden. Let stand for 5 minutes before serving.

INDIAN-SPICED
TACOS
with mango salsa
serves 4

If I had to choose one Mexican dish to dine out on for the rest of my life it would be tacos. It's the soft flour tortilla version that I really swoon over, even if it happens to be a little messy to eat. Here I've gone for an Indian-spiced filling that will really put a spring in your step—forget the chipotle; this dish is all about the garam masala… just the right side of smoky with the merest hint of sweet. Oh, and you can stop worrying about the sour cream, too. I've got you covered with a cashew version that will make your head spin…

INGREDIENTS

For the sour cream
1 cup cashews
juice of ½ lemon
1 teaspoon cider vinegar
salt and freshly ground
black pepper

For the salsa
1½ cups cherry or baby plum
tomatoes, quartered
½ mango, finely diced
½ red onion, finely diced
1 avocado, finely diced
¼ cup sweet corn
1 red chile, seeded and finely
chopped
juice of 1 lime, plus extra to serve
small bunch of cilantro, chopped

For the chickpeas
1 heaping teaspoon garam masala

METHOD

1 First, make the sour cream. Place the cashews in a bowl, completely cover with water, and soak for at least 6 hours.

2 Drain and rinse the cashews and place in a blender with ½ cup water, the lemon juice, cider vinegar, ½ teaspoon salt, and a grinding of black pepper. Process until smooth, occasionally scraping down the sides with a spatula—this will take about 5 minutes. Transfer to a bowl, cover, and store in the fridge until needed.

3 For the salsa, season the tomatoes with salt and combine with all the ingredients, apart from the cilantro, in a medium bowl. Add half the cilantro (reserve the remainder for serving), season, and stir well to combine. Cover and set aside.

4 Preheat the oven to 400°F. For the chickpeas, place the spices in a bowl with 1 teaspoon salt and ¼ teaspoon black pepper. Mix into a paste with the oil and agave. Drain and rinse the chickpeas and roll in the spice mixture until completely covered. Season well and transfer to a roasting pan. Roast in the oven for 20 to 30 minutes until crunchy. Season with a pinch more salt when they are removed from the oven—if not using immediately, cover with foil and keep warm in the turned-off oven.

INGREDIENTS

1 teaspoon ground cumin
¼ teaspoon paprika
¼ teaspoon ground cinnamon
seeds from 2 cardamom pods
3 tablespoons olive oil
¼ teaspoon agave nectar
2 × 14oz cans chickpeas
12 small flour tortillas

METHOD

5 Preheat a grill pan and warm each tortilla for 10 seconds on each side. Transfer to a heated plate and cover with a clean kitchen towel or foil to keep warm while the remaining tortillas are heated.

6 Place a small spoonful of cashew cream on each tortilla followed by some chickpeas, salsa, cilantro, and an additional spritz of lime. Fold and enjoy!

summertime STEW

serves 2 to 3

This summer stew involves very little standing over a hot stove ("Phew!" says you), and makes for a fabulous midweek meal that you can happily consume al fresco. Full of texture, it could easily be eaten on its own or with quinoa as a super-speedy supper. It also doubles up magnificently as an impromptu picnic dish served with chunks of crusty bread. The fresh, simple flavors are the main draw for me with the grilled sweet corn just adding that necessary barbecue edge. More of an assembly job than anything else, the recipe requires very little cooking skill, but the results are still impressive—my kind of dish. Take it one step further by doubling the quantities and serving it in one large bowl that everyone can dig into at a small summertime party… trust me, I've never had any complaints yet! Now, where's that glass of sangria?

INGREDIENTS

1 corn on the cob
1 tablespoon olive oil
2 large carrots, grated
1 red bell pepper, seeded and
roughly chopped
4 sun-dried tomatoes in oil,
drained
1 celery rib, roughly chopped
1 small red onion, finely diced
1 avocado, roughly chopped
juice of 1 lemon or lime
¾ cup basil leaves, roughly torn

For the dressing
juice of ½ lemon
2 tablespoons extra virgin olive oil
salt and freshly ground
black pepper

METHOD

1 Preheat a grill pan. Rub the sweet corn with the oil and cook in the grill pan for 15 minutes, turning occasionally, until slightly blackened. Carefully remove the sweet corn kernels from the cob using a sharp knife.

2 In a large bowl combine the carrots, red bell pepper, sun-dried tomatoes, celery, red onion, avocado, and grilled sweet corn. Drizzle with a little lemon or lime juice and gently stir through.

3 For the dressing, whisk together the lemon juice, extra virgin olive oil, and salt and pepper and pour over the stew. Finally stir in the basil and serve.

BEET, CITRUS, *and fennel* SALAD

serves 2 to 4

Beets are such an underused vegetable in my opinion. Full of flavor with an incredibly dense, satisfying texture, it is such a delicious base to any great salad. I've used a little sugar here to bring out the sweetness of the fruit and balance any sour notes that may interfere with the fennel, but feel free to leave it out if you prefer. Like beets, fennel is also the underdog of the slightly unusual "not quite sure what to do with it" vegetable world, which is why this dish is a champion of all that is great but often overlooked in our everyday eats.

INGREDIENTS

1 orange, peeled
1 grapefruit, peeled
1 lime, peeled
½ fennel bulb, very thinly sliced
or shaved
1 tablespoon agave nectar
⅓ cup mint, roughly chopped
4 small cooked beets,
sliced into rounds
salt and freshly ground
black pepper
1 tablespoon finely chopped fresh
flat-leaf parsley

METHOD

1 Segment the fruit into a large dish along with the shaved fennel. Squeeze out any excess juice into a separate bowl and whisk together with the agave to form a light dressing. Pour most of the dressing over the fruit and fennel, reserving a little for later. Toss in half the mint and set aside.

2 Layer the beets in a shallow dish. Sprinkle with a little salt and pepper as well as the chopped parsley.

3 Spoon the fennel and fruit over the beets and finish with the remaining dressing and a final scattering of mint.

zesty bulgur wheat and WATERMELON SALAD

serves 2 to 4

Bulgur wheat is often guilty of being a wee bit bland but this salad shows that all it requires is a little gentle coaxing to bring out its deeply nutty flavor. And while watermelon may seem like an odd choice in a savory dish (stay with me, fruit-phobes), it really does work fantastically well in balancing the zesty lime dressing with the spritely radish and scallion add-ins. Come summertime, this is the one recipe you'll be pulling out of your sleeve time and time again… just you wait and see.

INGREDIENTS

For the salad
1¾ cups bulgur wheat
grated zest and juice of 1 lime
salt
2 tablespoons extra virgin olive oil
1 teaspoon agave syrup
1 tablespoon cider vinegar
6 to 8 radishes, finely sliced
2 scallions, finely sliced
1 small celery rib, finely sliced
½ watermelon, seeded and cut into small bite-sized pieces
½ cup pumpkin seeds, toasted
⅓ cup mint leaves, chopped
large handful of China Rose radish sprouts, to garnish (optional)

METHOD

1 Place the bulgur wheat in a large bowl along with the lime zest. Lightly season with a little salt and stir to incorporate. Cover with 1 cup of freshly boiled water and place a plate or plastic wrap over the bowl. Let stand for at least 10 minutes or until all the water has been absorbed. Fluff with a fork. Set aside to cool, uncovered, for at least 15 minutes.

2 For the dressing, whisk together the lime juice, oil, agave syrup, cider vinegar, and a pinch of salt until it emulsifies. Set aside.

3 When the bulgur wheat has cooled, add the radishes, scallions, and celery. Stir and pour in the dressing, stirring again to ensure everything is coated. Toss in the melon, toasted pumpkin seeds, and finally the mint. Taste for seasoning and scatter with the China Rose radish sprouts, if using. Serve.

sweet potato and spinach
SUSHI

serves 2 to 4

When someone says sushi, do you automatically think fish? It's a natural link to make, yet the term itself is literally defined as "sour-tasting," which explains the crucial use of seasoning—or, at a push, the cider vinegar and sugar mix I have suggested as an alternative here. Of course, the fillings might be erring a tad on the Western side of things, but adapting cuisines has become par for the course these days, so I'm not at all embarrassed to serve up this version to friends for Sushi Night. You will need a rolling mat for this recipe.

INGREDIENTS

1 cup sushi rice
1 small sweet potato, unpeeled,
cut lengthwise into 4 to 5 pieces,
and cubed
soy sauce or tamari, to season
sesame oil, to season
2 tablespoons sushi rice seasoning
or 3 tablespoons cider vinegar
mixed with 1 teaspoon sugar
3 nori sheets
3 tablespoons sweet chili
dipping sauce
2 cups baby spinach, stalks
removed
1 avocado, peeled and sliced into
long strips (drizzle with 1 teaspoon
lemon juice to stop it discoloring)
²/₃ cup sesame seeds, toasted

METHOD

1 Preheat the oven to 400°F. Rinse the rice and place it in a pan, and cover with enough water to cook (check the package instructions). Set aside to soak for 30 minutes.

2 Place the potato cubes on a baking sheet, season with a little soy sauce and sesame oil, and bake in the oven for 20 minutes or until crisp on the outside, shaking the pan occasionally. Remove from the oven and set aside to cool.

3 Bring the rice and water to a boil, cover, and then cook according to the package instructions, until all the water has been absorbed. Transfer to a baking sheet and spread out to let it cool. When the sushi rice is cool, pour in the sushi rice seasoning or cider vinegar mix and stir thoroughly.

4 Place the first nori sheet on a rolling mat. Spread out a third of the rice over the nori sheet, leaving ½in or so gap at the top of the sheet, and pour over 1 tablespoon of the sweet chili sauce, spreading it with the back of a spoon, where you plan to place the first layer of filling.

5 At the bottom of the sheet place some spinach across the nori sheet until it overlaps at each end, add a layer of sweet potato, then some avocado. Using the mat, tightly roll the sheet using your fingers to tuck in the filling. Place the sushi roll on a wooden cutting board, ensuring the seam is underneath.

INGREDIENTS

To serve
sweet chili dipping sauce
soy sauce
wasabi

METHOD

6 For inside-out rolls, (it's easier if the mat is covered with plastic wrap), use the same method, spreading the sauce on top of the nori, then adding the rice, and turning the sushi over after you have secured the rice. Once you have filled a l the rolls, roll each one in a large plate of toasted sesame seeds.

7 To cut the rolls, fill a tall glass with water and wet a sharp knife. Cut about 8 medium-s zed slices from each roll, wetting the knife between each slice. Serve the sushi with sweet chili sauce, soy sauce, and wasabi.

~ strawberry ~
MARGARITA

serves 2

Margaritas spell summer to me. Long, hot days with ice cold drinks, it really doesn't get much better than that… particularly when those beverages contain tequila! I like my cocktails to pack a punch and this simple strawberry margarita teeters right on the edge of being "knock your socks off" strong and soothingly refreshing. Perhaps it's just as well I haven't listed the measurements for a pitcher, eh?

INGREDIENTS

8 strawberries, hulled
3 to 4 ice cubes
¼ cup tequila
2 tablespoons Cointreau or triple sec
juice of 2 limes
1 tablespoon agave nectar or sugar syrup

To decorate
1 teaspoon sea salt
1 teaspoon sugar
juice and grated zest of 1 lime
2 lime slices

METHOD

1 Put the strawberries into a hand-held blender and process until puréed. Press the purée through a sieve to remove the seeds.

2 Put the ice cubes into a cocktail shaker along with the tequila, Cointreau, lime juice, agave nectar or sugar syrup and strawberry purée.

3 Shake it vigorously until the outside of the shaker frosts up.

4 Place the salt, sugar, and lime zest in a small bowl and mix well to combine. Transfer the mixture to a plate. Place the lime juice in another small bowl and dip the rim of two cocktail glasses in the juice. Invert each glass onto the plate and twist the glass until the rim is coated in the salt-and-sugar mixture.

5 Turn the glasses the right way up and carefully pour in the margarita (avoiding the rims of the glasses). Decorate with a slice of lime and serve.

cherry ginger FIZZ

serves 2

My love of cocktails seriously knows no bounds. Whether it be rum, gin, or vodka (and I'm even partial to the odd drop of tequila), the many and varied concoctions I have tried over the years remains countless. Anything and everything, this mixer and that—you name it, I've tried it; but there is something so sweetly satisfying about Bourbon… particularly when mixed with ginger. This, then, is that self-same classic combo with just enough of a twist to keep it interesting. Even though the cherry might seem like a very girly addition, I've never seen a guy turn it down yet.

INGREDIENTS

¼ cup Bourbon
2 tablespoons cherry brandy
⅓ cup pomegranate juice
juice of ½ lime
4 ice cubes
⅓ cup ginger ale
2 maraschino cherries, to decorate

METHOD

1 Place all the ingredients except for the ginger ale and cherries in a cocktail shaker and shake vigorously for a minute or so until thoroughly mixed.

2 Pour into 2 chilled cocktail glasses, top with ginger ale, and adorn each with a cherry.

hitchcock blonde COCKTAIL

serves 1

Being somewhat of a Hitchcock obsessive I've always fancied myself as one of those (what I imagine to be) gin-drinking blondes that ooze sophistication from every one of their screen-siren pores... even though I'm neither blonde nor possess Janet's or Tippi's beguiling ways. Regardless, this cocktail does go some way to making me feel a bit old-school Hollywood, if only for the length of time it takes me to drink one—and then promptly make another, ahem.

INGREDIENTS

2 to 3 ice cubes
3 tablespoons gin
1 tablespoon grenadine
juice of ½ lemon
3 tablespoons freshly squeezed
grapefruit juice
grapefruit segments, to serve

METHOD

1 Put a cocktail glass in the freezer for at least 30 minutes to chill.

2 Place the ice cubes in a cocktail shaker and pour in the gin, grenadine, lemon juice, and grapefruit juice. Shake vigorously until you can no longer hear the ice cubes clanging against the sides.

3 Place the grapefruit segments in the chilled glass and pour in the cocktail.

Sides & SAUCES

CRUSTY NO-KNEAD CARROT AND
ZUCCHINI BREAD

TEAR 'N' SHARE ANTIPASTI
FOCACCIA

PECAN-TOPPED
BAKED SWEET POTATO

PISTACHIO, PARSLEY, AND
WALNUT PESTO

PESTO-ROASTED BROCCOLI

SALT 'N' PEPPER TOFU FINGERS

GRILLED POLENTA STICKS

PAN-FRIED PAPRIKA-SPICED SPROUTS

CUMIN-SPICED CARROTS

BRAISED RED CABBAGE WITH APPLE

TARRAGON, PEA, AND SPINACH SIDE

GREEN BEAN SALAD WITH LEMON,
GARLIC, AND CHILE

SIMPLE POTATO SALAD

POTATO DAUPHINOISE

EASY DRESSING

MAPLE MUSTARD SALAD DRESSING

HUMMUS SAUCE

AVOCADO SAUCE

TAPENADE

VEGAN RAITA

CREAMY EGGPLANT DIP

THICK 'N' CREAMY HUMMUS

TWO-STEP TOMATO SAUCE

EASY VEGAN GRAVY

CINNAMON CITRUS CRANBERRY
SAUCE

SPICED PUMPKIN BUTTER

CRUSTY NO-KNEAD
carrot and zucchini
BREAD

makes 1 × 1lb loaf

Bread making can often cause the most confident of cooks to tremble at the knees. All that yeast activating, kneading, resting (and not to mention waiting!) is enough to send anyone straight to the supermarket shelf to grab a loaf of the white stuff… and who can blame 'em? Luckily not all breads are created equally—and some involve even less effort than choosing a store-bought batch from your local bakery. This crusty no-knead carrot and zucchini version is one such recipe that requires nothing more than throwing everything together in a bowl and having enough patience to let it bake for the mere 30 minutes it will take to turn miraculously into one of the easiest breads you could possibly muster.

INGREDIENTS

1²⁄₃ cups all-purpose flour, plus extra for dusting
¾ cup whole wheat flour
1 teaspoon baking powder
¾ teaspoon baking soda
pinch of sugar
1 teaspoon dried thyme, plus extra for sprinkling
salt and freshly ground black pepper
1 carrot, grated
1 zucchini, grated
¾ cup plant milk, such as soy, almond, or oat
½ cup walnuts, roughly chopped
2 tablespoons mixed seeds, plus extra for sprinkling
hummus, to serve (optional)

METHOD

1 Preheat the oven to 400°F.

2 Mix the dry ingredients in a large bowl with ½ teaspoon salt and set aside. Squeeze the grated carrot and zucchini to remove any excess liquid and season with a little pepper. Add the carrot and zucchini mix to the dry ingredients and stir well.

3 Make a well in the center and pour in the plant milk, and then gently fold using a spatula, ensuring not to overwork the mixture. Stir in the walnuts and seeds.

4 Dust a little flour over a work surface and a baking sheet. Turn the mixture onto the surface and shape into a rough oval about 12in in diameter.

5 Transfer the dough to the baking sheet, score the top with a sharp, floured knife, and sprinkle with a little more salt, thyme, and extra seeds.

6 Lightly dust the loaf with flour and bake for 30 minutes or until it sounds hollow when you tap the bottom. Let it cool on a wire rack for a few minutes before slicing or tearing. Serve warm and generously spread with hummus.

tear 'n' share antipasti
FOCACCIA

serves 4 to 6

There is something so impressive about a home-baked loaf, and nothing makes guests feel more welcome than fluffy fresh foccacia ready for sharing. Almost a meal in itself, this recipe is a terrific way to entertain the easy way. Forget time-consuming nibbles and all that other stress-inducing stuff; just put your energy into one great hunk of antipasti-clad bread and you'll keep your guests more than happy until the main course arrives. It's casual, interactive, and, best of all, tastes incredible… no one will even notice there isn't an appetizer on your menu.

INGREDIENTS

2½ cups bread flour, plus extra
for dusting
1 teaspoon salt
1 tablespoon sugar
¼oz package active dried yeast
4 to 5 tablespoons olive oil, plus
extra for greasing

For the topping
1 to 1½ cups mixed antipasti,
such as sundried tomatoes, olives,
grilled eggplant, artichokes,
mushrooms
¾ cup fresh thyme sprigs,
leaves removed
sea salt
extra virgin olive oil, for drizzling

METHOD

1 Combine the flour, salt, sugar, and yeast in a large bowl. Pour ½ cup lukewarm water into a large measuring cup and stir in the oil. Make a well in the center of the flour and pour in a little of the water and oil mixture. Using your hands (or a spatula if you prefer), gradually mix the flour into the water until a dough is formed, adding more water as required. Add a little more flour if it is too sticky or more water if it is too dry.

2 Turn the dough onto a floured surface and knead for 10 to 15 minutes until it is smooth and elastic. Oil the bowl and return the dough to it. Cover with a clean damp cloth and let it rise for 1½ hours.

3 Preheat the oven to 375°F. Oil a 15in pan or baking sheet.

4 Transfer the dough to the pan or sheet and gently press it out so it fits the shape. Cover with the cloth and let it rise for another 10 to 15 minutes.

5 Dimple the dough with your fingers and dot the antipasti across the surface, pressing it in lightly. Sprinkle the thyme leaves and sea salt over the bread and drizzle generously with extra virgin olive oil. Bake the bread in the oven for 25 to 30 minutes or until it is perfectly golden on top and sounds hollow when tapped on the bottom. Cool slightly on a wire rack and serve while still warm. This will keep for a day or two.

pecan-topped BAKED SWEET POTATO

serves 6 to 8

I discovered the delights of Thanksgiving dinner when we briefly lived in the States, and this dish in particular has really stayed with me since. Normally it's topped with marshmallows and, although there are some fantastic vegan marshmallows now on the market, that addition is a sweet step too far even for me. The pecans lend a terrific crunch, and the maple syrup is a perfect pairing with the sweet potato—it just remains to be seen if you can put your sweet and savory reservations to one side, so you can appreciate the joyous nature of this wickedly indulgent, savory side dish.

INGREDIENTS

2 large sweet potatoes
1 tablespoon olive oil
salt and freshly ground
black pepper
2 tablespoons soy milk (or other plant milk)
2 tablespoons vegan butter
1 teaspoon vanilla extract
¼ teaspoon ground cinnamon
¼ teaspoon freshly grated nutmeg

For the topping
¼ cup pecans, chopped
1½ tablespoons maple syrup
1 tablespoon all-purpose flour
2 tablespoons vegan butter

METHOD

1 Preheat the oven to 400°F.

2 Prick the sweet potatoes all over with a fork and rub them with the olive oil, salt, and pepper. Place directly onto the oven shelf and bake for at least 1 hour until the skin is soft. Remove the potatoes from the oven and set aside to cool. Reduce the oven temperature to 350°F.

3 Halve the potatoes and scoop the flesh into a medium mixing bowl. Season with salt and pepper, add the soy milk, vegan butter, vanilla extract, cinnamon, and nutmeg and roughly mash—it's good to keep a little texture in there.

4 In a separate bowl, mix together all the topping ingredients, reserving half of the butter.

5 Transfer the mashed sweet potato to a 7in baking dish and spread evenly using a spatula. Sprinkle with the pecan crumble topping and dot with the rest of the butter. Bake in the oven for 30 to 40 minutes and serve hot.

PISTACHIO, PARSLEY, *and walnut* PESTO

makes approximately 1 cup

You may think that pesto requires Parmesan in order to be delicious, but I am here to tell you that cheese is not the crucial element in this most famous of Italian sauces… contrary to popular belief. Toasting the nuts will maximize their flavor and texture, and the parsley is a nice twist on the usual basil without being overpowering. Pesto is no longer off limits to vegans and, best of all, it can be whipped up in a matter of minutes. It's so versatile, too: stir it into pasta, potatoes, or beans or use it as a spread in sandwiches.

INGREDIENTS

¾ cup pistachios
½ cup walnuts
2½ cups fresh flat-leaf parsley
juice of 1 lemon
3 garlic cloves
generous pinch of freshly
grated nutmeg
¾ cup extra virgin olive oil
1 teaspoon sea salt,
plus extra to taste
freshly ground black pepper

METHOD

1 Heat a small, non-stick, heavy-bottomed frying pan and lightly toast the pistachios over medium heat for several minutes, shaking the pan frequently. Let them cool a little before transferring them to a food processor. Repeat to toast the walnuts and set aside.

2 Process the pistachios into fine crumbs before adding the toasted walnuts and blending for a few seconds more. Add the parsley, lemon juice, garlic, nutmeg, half the olive oil, and the sea salt and process thoroughly until a thick paste has formed.

3 Scrape down the sides of the blender, season to taste with black pepper and extra salt if desired, add the remaining oil, and process again until you achieve a coarse, pesto-like sauce. This will keep, refrigerated, for up to 1 week.

pesto-roasted BROCCOLI

serves 2 to 4

You could use my Pistachio, Parsley, and Walnut Pesto for this dish (page 119), but for a speedier option, it's great that supermarkets are now stocking everyday vegan options such as pesto. Not only does it make life a little simpler, it also means you can create this impressive, easy side in a flash… allowing you to focus on the main event or fuss over your extravagant dessert. Nutritional yeast (or "nooch" as it is often affectionately known) might not be so readily available, but most health stores should sell it and it really does add something to the finished dish, as well as giving you a necessary (and delicious) B12 boost, so sprinkle with abandon. Us vegans do have to be mindful of our B12 intake, as it's not so readily available in plant food, so it's always wise to supplement… you don't want to be compromising on your brain and nervous-system health, which is why I sprinkle nooch on just about everything. Well, a girl can never be too careful, can she?

INGREDIENTS

1 heaping tablespoon vegan pesto
juice of ½ lemon
2 tablespoons olive oil
1 large head of broccoli
(about 1lb), cut into medium florets
salt and freshly ground
black pepper
nutritional yeast or toasted pine
nuts, to serve

METHOD

1 Preheat the oven to 350°F.

2 Whisk the pesto, lemon juice, and oil together in a small bowl. Place the broccoli florets in a roasting pan. Lightly season with salt and pepper, then pour in the pesto dressing and toss until the broccoli is thoroughly coated. Roast in the oven for 20 to 25 minutes or until tender, shaking the pan occasionally,

3 Serve warm with a sprinkling of nutritional yeast or a smattering of toasted pine nuts.

salt 'n' pepper TOFU FINGERS

serves 2 to 4

Do you think take-out-style tofu is unachievable in your own kitchen? Well, this recipe is the ultimate remedy for all those cravings that involve crunchy bean curd, of which, in my world, there are many. It took me a while to figure out the crucial step in getting that outer coating perfectly crisp, but once I discovered it was just a matter of coating each finger in cornstarch, there really was no going back. For a more intense salt 'n' pepper flavor, I like to dredge them in these seasonings prior to coating each finger in cornstarch… also, you could try skewering them for a fun finger-food option at parties.

INGREDIENTS

14oz firm tofu
1 tablespoon sea salt
1 tablespoon black peppercorns
4 to 5 tablespoons cornstarch
sunflower oil, for frying
sweet chili or satay sauce, to serve

METHOD

1 Drain the tofu and press out any excess water—place it in a shallow bowl, rest a plate on top, and place 2 × 14oz food cans on the plate. Set aside for 20 minutes, drain the tofu again, and pat dry with a clean kitchen towel. Halve the tofu lengthwise and then quarter each piece to get 8 symmetrical fingers.

2 Crush the sea salt and pepper in a mortar and pestle and transfer to a plate. Dredge each tofu finger in the salt and pepper mixture.

3 Lightly season the cornstarch and place on a plate. Coat each tofu piece in the cornstarch.

4 Pour about ½in of sunflower oil into a small, heavy-bottomed frying pan and place over medium heat. Fry the tofu pieces in batches until golden and crunchy on all sides. They retain their heat very well, so just keep them loosely covered in foil while frying the remaining batches.

5 Drain on paper towels and serve hot with a sweet chili or satay sauce for dipping.

grilled
POLENTA STICKS

serves 4

Polenta is such a wonderfully versatile ingredient that I often use it in baking and cooking. But this is definitely my favorite way to use it. I find that frying can sometimes render the sticks a soggy mess... and besides, grilling is a much healthier way to enjoy them because you require only the merest smidge of oil. In my opinion these are best served with a spoonful of Two-step Tomato Sauce (see page 138) and some lightly sautéed spinach seasoned with a little nutmeg. In this case, simple really is best.

INGREDIENTS

1 vegetable bouillon cube
1¼ cups polenta
1 tablespoon olive oil
salt and freshly ground
black pepper

METHOD

1 Line a 2lb loaf pan with plastic wrap.

2 Bring 3 cups water to a rolling boil, crumble in the bouillon cube, and stir to dissolve. Pour in the polenta, whisking vigorously to avoid clumping, and simmer until it thickens. Cook over low heat for around 20 minutes, stirring frequently to prevent it from sticking. When the texture becomes thick and rubbery, transfer it to the lined pan. Spread evenly using a spatula, wrap tightly in the plastic wrap, and refrigerate overnight.

3 Invert the loaf pan onto a cutting board and unwrap the polenta. Slice it into sticks—you should get around 12, depending on thickness.

4 Heat a grill pan over medium heat. Brush each stick with a little olive oil, season with salt and pepper, and grill in two batches for 7 to 10 minutes until browned and marked on each side. They retain their heat well, so just cover the first cooked batch with foil while you grill the remainder. Drain on paper towels and serve hot.

pan-fried paprika-spiced SPROUTS

serves 2 to 4

Love them or loathe them, Brussels sprouts are a great addition to any holiday meal. I'm firmly in the "obsessed" camp, which is why I've taken to eating them right through winter in many varied ways. Roasted, boiled, steamed, (and even raw)—you name it, I've tried it—but I keep coming back to this pan-fried version that is teeming with flavor and so easy to achieve. Don't feel the need to restrict it to holidays though; use it liberally as a topping to curries, filling for quesadillas, or even on its own with a side of rice. You might think you hate them, but I urge you to sample sprouts sliced and fried before you wholly make up your mind.

INGREDIENTS

2 to 3 tablespoons olive oil
2 shallots, finely sliced
salt and freshly ground
black pepper
2 garlic cloves, finely sliced
2½ cups Brussels sprouts,
finely sliced
1 heaping teaspoon ground cumin
1 heaping teaspoon
smoked paprika
½ cup fresh flat-leaf parsley,
roughly chopped
1 tablespoon sesame seeds, toasted

METHOD

1 Heat 2 tablespoons of the oil in a medium-sized, non-stick, heavy-bottomed frying pan. Add the shallots, season with salt and pepper, and gently cook for a few minutes. Add the garlic and cook gently for 1 to 2 minutes, ensuring it doesn't brown.

2 Add the sprouts to the pan and cook for several minutes, adding a little more oil if necessary. Sprinkle with the cumin and smoked paprika. Mix thoroughly and cook for 5 minutes or until the sprouts are just tender.

3 Add the parsley to the pan, season, and stir. Sprinkle with the sesame seeds just before serving.

cumin—spiced
CARROTS

serves 2 to 4

The spices of the Middle East and North Africa really have a hold of my palate. Granted, this might not be an entirely authentic recipe, but it goes some way in satisfying that need for sweet and savory together in one harmonious mouthful… so much so I could seriously consume a bowlful by itself. If you're slightly less uncouth than I am, you might be inclined to serve it as a side to any number of dishes, such as fragrant couscous, vegetable tagine, or even simple lemon-infused rice. For a colorful variation, I like to use heritage carrots in purples and pale yellows—but if you're using a mixture of purple and non-purple varieties, you'll need to boil them separately in the first step of this recipe to keep the colors from bleeding.

INGREDIENTS

5 carrots, sliced thinly
on a diagonal
1 tablespoon olive oil
¾ tablespoon vegan butter
salt and freshly ground
black pepper
1 heaping teaspoon ground cumin
¼ teaspoon ground coriander
pinch of ground cinnamon
1 teaspoon agave nectar or
pomegranate molasses
½ cup fresh flat-leaf parsley,
roughly chopped
extra virgin olive oil, to serve

METHOD

1 Bring a small saucepan of water to a boil. Add the sliced carrots to the pan. (Remember, if you're using a mixture of purple and non-purple heritage varieties, you'll need to boil them in separate pans). Simmer gently until just soft but still retaining some bite—around 5 minutes. Drain and set aside.

2 Heat the oil and butter in a small, non-stick saucepan, add the carrots, season with salt and pepper, and gently stir to coat. Sprinkle in the spices and agave nectar. Mix thoroughly and cook through over gentle heat for a few more minutes until the spices begin to exude an aroma.

3 Taste for seasoning and stir in most of the parsley. Serve sprinkled with the remaining parsley and a generous drizzle of extra virgin olive oil.

BRAISED RED
cabbage with
APPLE

serves 6 to 8

This festive side is a classic British dish that I never fail to make around Christmas—although there's really no reason why it can't be enjoyed all year round too. Slow-cooked over low heat, the aroma alone is enough to bring a smile to my festive-loving face, so it's just as well the taste lives up to its magnificent scent. There is a fine line between the cabbage being tender and turning into mush, however, so make sure you keep the heat low and stir frequently to prevent burning. It's also a terrific dish to make the day before… always welcome when you're cooking for groups! Simply reheat for around 10 to 15 minutes and serve hot alongside your favorite vegan main course.

INGREDIENTS

1 tablespoon sunflower oil

1 red onion, roughly chopped

salt and freshly ground
black pepper

1 red cabbage, thinly sliced

1 tablespoon red wine vinegar

2 Granny Smith apples, peeled,
cored, and chopped into
medium chunks

¼ cup granulated sugar

¼ teaspoon freshly grated nutmeg

¼ teaspoon ground allspice

1 star anise

1 cinnamon stick

pomegranate seeds and chopped
fresh flat-leaf parsley, to serve

METHOD

1 Heat the oil in a large, heavy-bottomed saucepan. Add the onion to the pan, season with salt and pepper, and sweat for several minutes until it begins to soften.

2 Add the cabbage to the pan, stir to incorporate, and add the red wine vinegar, as well as a little more seasoning. Cover and sweat for several minutes. Add the apples, sugar, nutmeg, allspice, star anise, and cinnamon stick. Season again and stir thoroughly. Cook, covered, over low heat, for around 2 hours, until the cabbage is very tender, stirring occasionally and adding a little water if it starts to stick.

3 Discard the star anise and cinnamon stick, taste for seasoning, and serve sprinkled with pomegranate seeds and chopped flat-leaf parsley.

TARRAGON
pea and spinach side

serves 2 to 4

Tarragon's aniseedy overtones can make it a tricky customer when it comes to adding it to certain dishes, ensuring its well secured place in the "underused herb of choice" category. However, when it works, it works (and I must concede to having a soft spot for its distinctly pungent taste), making this side a great example of this unique perennial herb becoming the unequivocal star of the show. As I mention in the recipe, the cream addition is optional (and I honestly like it equally both ways), although I often go down the more calorific route if I have guests, just because it makes the dish feel more special.

INGREDIENTS

1 tablespoon olive oil
1 onion, finely chopped
1 garlic clove, finely chopped
½ cup tarragon leaves,
finely chopped
salt and freshly ground
black pepper
1 vegetable bouillon cube
1¾ cups frozen peas
7oz spinach
¼ teaspoon freshly grated nutmeg
½ cup soy or oat cream (optional)

METHOD

1 Heat the oil in a large frying pan and lightly cook the onion until it begins to soften. Add the garlic, chopped tarragon, and a little salt and pepper, and cook for a few minutes longer before crumbling in the bouillon cube and adding the peas and enough water just to cover the vegetables.

2 Bring to a gentle simmer and, when the peas have thawed and the stock has reduced, add the spinach and nutmeg and let the spinach wilt.

3 If you're not adding the cream, season the vegetables generously with black pepper and serve. Otherwise add the soy cream and a little black pepper and allow it to gently heat through. Serve as an interesting side at a vegetarian Sunday dinner.

GREEN BEAN SALAD
with lemon, garlic, and chile

serves 2 to 4

Green beans are just about my favorite vegetable—or at the very least, figure in my top five. If in doubt, I will always, without fail, serve these long-limbed beauties with just about every dish I cook... from spaghetti to tofu and beyond. Perhaps it's their inoffensive manner and playful appearance (who needs a fork when you have fingers?) but they seem to go down just as well with children and adults alike—no mean feat. This recipe certainly errs on the more grown-up side, though, with the addition of chile, lemon, and the not-so-universally-loved caper. They've always been the singular sticking point between myself and one of my all-time favorite heroines (and enthusiastic foodie herself), the late Nora Ephron. Nora may have hated the little buggers, but on this one, very small matter, I'm afraid I just can't agree—plus, I fear that, if absent here, the capers would be rather sorely missed, so I'm afraid they must, must stay. Sorry, Nora!

INGREDIENTS

2 cups green beans, trimmed
1 tablespoon olive oil
4 scallions, thickly sliced
½ to 1 red chile, finely sliced,
with seeds
2 to 3 garlic cloves, finely sliced
salt and freshly ground
black pepper
grated zest and juice of ½ lemon
1 tablespoon capers in brine,
drained, rinsed, and chopped
1 tablespoon chopped fresh
flat-leaf parsley

METHOD

1 Bring a medium-sized saucepan of water to a boil and blanch the green beans for a few minutes until just tender—be careful not to overcook them as they'll lose their color and get soggy. Immediately drain and place in a pan of iced water or run under a very cold tap for 1 to 2 minutes.

2 Heat the olive oil in a small frying pan. Add the scallions, chile, and garlic and lightly cook for 1 to 2 minutes. Season with salt and pepper, remove from the heat, and let cool.

3 Halve the green beans by cutting diagonally and transfer to a large bowl. Season and stir in the lemon zest and juice, capers, parsley, and scallion mixture. Season to taste and lightly toss until coated in the mixture.

4 Eat immediately or refrigerate to serve later.

~ simple ~
POTATO SALAD

serves 4 to 6

Potato salad doesn't need to contain mayo. Even though there are some wonderful vegan mayonnaise options now on the market, I still prefer this lighter homemade dressing. The gherkins and celery give a wonderful crunch, and, even though I'm fully aware of some people's aversion to capers, I fully stand by their addition to this dish. So, step away from the mayo and get your salad-dressing groove on instead.

INGREDIENTS

12 to 15 salad potatoes, such as fingerling, scrubbed
salt and freshly ground black pepper
2 scallions, finely chopped
2 celery ribs, finely chopped
3 pickled gherkins, drained and finely chopped
2 tablespoons capers in brine, drained, rinsed and finely chopped
¾ cup fresh flat-leaf parsley, finely chopped

For the dressing
2 heaping teaspoons Dijon mustard
1 tablespoon cider vinegar
juice of ½ lemon
1 teaspoon agave nectar
¼ cup olive oil

METHOD

1 Place the potatoes in a large pan of salted water and bring to a boil. Cook for around 15 minutes or until tender, drain, and set aside to cool. When they are completely cool, halve each potato, season with salt and pepper, and transfer to a large serving bowl.

2 Put all the dressing ingredients with some seasoning in a lidded screwtop jar and shake well until the dressing emulsifies. Alternatively, whisk the ingredients in a bowl.

3 Add the scallions, celery, gherkins, and capers to the potato bowl and pour in the dressing, using a spatula to carefully incorporate the ingredients. Stir the parsley through the salad. Taste for seasoning and chill in the fridge until ready to serve.

potato DAUPHINOISE

serves 4

I try not to rely too heavily on soy products, but in this instance I'm happy to go all out and indulge in a mammoth amount of plant-based cream—look away now, diet fiends! If you're allergic to soy (or simply want to avoid it), you can substitute coconut or even oat cream, but I would urge you to include the freshly grated nutmeg, as it really adds a certain something to this already über decadent side dish. Whoever said veganism equals deprivation quite clearly has never tasted this.

INGREDIENTS

vegan butter, for greasing
4 large potatoes (about 1lb 10oz),
cut into ¼in slices
salt and freshly ground
black pepper
1 garlic clove, finely chopped
1¼ cups soy cream
¼ teaspoon freshly grated nutmeg

METHOD

1 Preheat the oven to 350°F. Grease an 8in baking dish with vegan butter.

2 Arrange a layer of potatoes on the bottom of the dish, season with salt and pepper, sprinkle with a third of the garlic, drizzle with a third of the cream, and top with some of the grated nutmeg. Repeat these layers twice more.

3 Place the dish on a baking sheet and cover with foil. Bake in the oven for 1 hour, then remove the foil and bake uncovered for another 30 minutes.

SALAD DRESSINGS in SECONDS

both serve 2 to 3

I hate store-bought salad dressings. Where I'm happy to compromise on other things I just won't budge when it comes to what I put on my leaves—and those (usually) synthetic-tasting flavors just don't cut it. The terrific thing about these dressings is that you can vary them when it comes to the citrus and vinegar… you could try lime juice and white wine vinegar or clementine juice and cider vinegar for a slight variation on the basic recipes, and match it to the elements on your salad plate. Get shaking!

EASY DRESSING

1 teaspoon Dijon mustard
juice of ½ lemon
1 teaspoon red wine vinegar
1 teaspoon agave nectar or other sweetener
3 tablespoons extra virgin olive oil
salt and freshly ground black pepper

❚ Put all the ingredients in a lidded screwtop jar and shake vigorously until the dressing emulsifies.

MAPLE MUSTARD SALAD DRESSING

1 heaping teaspoon whole-grain mustard
juice of 1 lemon
1 tablespoon cider vinegar
1 tablespoon maple syrup
2 tablespoons olive oil
salt and freshly ground black pepper

❚ Put all the ingredients in a lidded screwtop jar and shake vigorously until the dressing emulsifies.

Variations

Jazz up your dressing with extra ingredients such as finely chopped garlic, scallions, capers, or chopped fresh herbs.

SIMPLE SAUCES in SECONDS

all serve 2 to 3

Quick fixes are just one way to take a meal from good to great in seconds, and these easy sauces are a terrific remedy when finishing off a dish with a little pizzazz. Drizzled over couscous, dolloped in pasta, stirred through salads, or spread over toast, there's a multitude of ways to enjoy any one of them…

HUMMUS SAUCE

2/3 cup hummus
juice of 1/2 lemon
freshly ground black pepper

▯ Place the hummus and lemon juice in a small bowl and stir well until smooth and runny. Season generously with black pepper, stir, and serve.

AVOCADO SAUCE

1 avocado
3 tablespoons plain soy yogurt
juice of 1 lime
salt and freshly ground black pepper

▯ Place everything in a bowl and process with a hand-held electric blender until completely smooth. Season to taste.

TAPENADE

2 cups pitted green olives
1 garlic clove
1/4 cup extra virgin olive oil
juice of 1/2 lemon
freshly ground black pepper

▯ Place everything in a bowl and process with a hand-held electric blender until coarse but spreadable. Season to taste.

VEGAN RAITA

1/2 cucumber, halved, seeded and grated
3/4 cup plain soy yogurt or coconut cream
juice of 1/2 lemon
salt and freshly ground black pepper

▯ Combine all the ingredients in a small dish, season with salt and pepper, cover, and chill in the fridge.

creamy eggplant DIP

serves 2 to 4

Eggplants are an obsession of mine. I just love that unctuously soft flesh and especially the rich dips that can be made from it. Forgive the "smoked" shortcut. I don't have the patience to hover over a flame for 20 minutes, so have popped a little smoked paprika in, which goes some way to giving the dip that requisite flavor. Well, we all have our kitchen limitations, don't we?

INGREDIENTS

oil, for greasing
2 eggplants
1 garlic clove
½ teaspoon sea salt
2 tablespoons extra virgin olive oil, plus extra for drizzling
juice of 1 lemon
¼ teaspoon smoked paprika
¼ cup tahini
½ cup fresh flat-leaf parsley, roughly chopped, plus extra to garnish
salt and freshly ground black pepper
toasted sesame seeds, to garnish

METHOD

1 Preheat the oven to 350°F. Oil a baking sheet.

2 Slice the eggplants lengthwise and place them on the baking sheet. Bake for 30 to 40 minutes until the flesh is soft, turning them over halfway through.

3 Cover and cool completely before scooping out the flesh. Chop thoroughly with a knife and then mash with a fork, ensuring there are no lumps.

4 Pound the garlic and sea salt together using a mortar and pestle.

5 Place the eggplant flesh in a bowl along with the crushed garlic, extra virgin olive oil, lemon juice, and smoked paprika. Mix thoroughly before stirring in the tahini and parsley.

6 Season with salt and pepper to taste and serve topped with a generous drizzle of extra virgin oil, a little more parsley, and a sprinkling of toasted sesame seeds. This is lovely served with crackers, pita, crudités or as a spread in sandwiches.

thick 'n' creamy
HUMMUS

serves 2 to 4

Once you read the method for this hummus recipe, you'll probably be wondering why on earth anyone would go to the bother of cooking "already cooked" canned chickpeas. Using canned chickpeas cuts out all that overnight soaking malarkey, which, in any case, is no good when you have a last minute hummus emergency—whatcha gonna do then, eh? The result of cooking the canned chickpeas is this surprisingly thick, rich, and creamy hummus. The texture and flavor are the closest thing you can get to the Middle East with a can of chickpeas from your local supermarket. Just doing my part for the corner cutters of the world!

INGREDIENTS

1 × 14oz can chickpeas,
drained and rinsed
2 garlic cloves
3 tablespoons tahini
juice of 2 lemons
sea salt

To serve
1 tablespoon extra virgin olive oil
¼ teaspoon smoked paprika

METHOD

1 Place the chickpeas in a pan and cover with about 2 cups water. Bring to a boil and simmer for 30 minutes. Reserve several tablespoons of the cooking liquid, drain the chickpeas, and rinse. Rub the skin off each chickpea (this is a crucial step) and rinse again.

2 Blend the chickpeas in a food processor until a smooth paste is formed.

3 Mash the garlic cloves with 1 teaspoon sea salt in a mortar and pestle until puréed.

4 Add most of the tahini, half of the lemon juice, and the garlic purée to the chickpeas and blend until smooth. If the mixture is still really thick, add a tablespoon or so of the reserved cooking liquid, a little more lemon juice, a touch more salt, and blend until you achieve a thick, creamy consistency.

5 Taste for seasoning—at this point you may want to add the remaining tahini, lemon juice, or a smidge more salt. Blend it for another minute or two.

6 Transfer the hummus to a shallow bowl and make a groove in the top using the back of a spoon. Generously drizzle over some extra virgin olive oil and finally add a light dusting of smoked paprika. Serve with pita or crudités.

two-step
TOMATO SAUCE

serves 2 to 4

This is such a simple yet effective sauce to have up your sleeve. No need to chop onions or labor over the stove… simply let the garlic do all the hard work and enjoy the rich tomato rewards. Serve over pasta, on pizza, in lasagna, or in other baked dishes requiring a tomato-based sauce. Or use it as a base for a multitude of other cuisines—add chopped fresh chiles for a Mexican twist or cinnamon for a Greek-style sauce. It's the ultimate minimal-fuss, maximum-flavor recipe that I use more often than I care to admit, and one I'm sure you'll find as invaluable as I do. If you want to prepare a larger quantity and freeze some, just double up.

INGREDIENTS

¼ cup olive oil
4 garlic cloves, finely chopped
1 × 14oz can plum tomatoes
salt and freshly ground
black pepper
pinch of sugar
½ teaspoon dried chile flakes
(optional)

METHOD

1 Heat the oil in a large, heavy-bottomed saucepan over low heat. Add the garlic to the pan and cook gently for several minutes, ensuring it does not brown.

2 Add the tomatoes and crush with the back of a spoon. Season with salt and pepper, add the sugar and chile flakes, if using, and stir well. Simmer over medium heat, covered, for 30 to 40 minutes, stirring occasionally and adding a little water from time to time. Taste for seasoning and serve.

easy vegan GRAVY

serves 2 to 4

I have several gravy recipes that I rely on quite heavily but this is by far the most straightforward. And while some of you may be recoiling in horror at the thought of putting marmite in, well, anything, may I be so bold as to urge you to put your reservations momentarily aside and give this frequently contentious ingredient a second chance? Whether you love it or loathe it you will absolutely notice a difference if you choose to omit it, as it lends a wonderful depth to the gravy that is difficult to replicate with anything else—and I promise the sauce will not be spoiled by an overriding yeast extract taste. Then it's just a case of throwing it all in a pan, whisking it together, and you're good to go... great with mashed potatoes, cauliflower, and vegan pies, it's basically a one-stop shop for all your vegan gravy needs!

INGREDIENTS

2 tablespoons all-purpose flour
1 tablespoon vegetable stock
granules
1 tablespoon soy sauce
1 tablespoon red wine vinegar
1 tablespoon Marmite
1 teaspoon agave nectar

METHOD

1 Place all the ingredients and 1¾ cups water in a shallow pan and whisk together.

2 Bring to a gentle boil and keep whisking until there are no lumps. Turn down the heat and allow the sauce to simmer and thicken for around 5 to 10 minutes, stirring frequently.

3 If the gravy isn't as thick as you'd like, add a little more flour and whisk vigorously to incorporate. If it is too thick, whisk in a little water.

CINNAMON CITRUS
cranberry
SAUCE

serves 4 to 6

While I'm not totally adverse to store-bought sauces, I really do prefer a homemade cranberry one at Christmas. This version is zingy and sweet in equal proportions, and the perfect addition to any dinner—or, my preference, a giant sandwich! It doesn't really matter whether your cranberries are fresh or frozen, and although you can leave it as chunky or smooth as you wish, I tend to keep several whole cranberries in there for texture. Either way, it's a deliciously straightforward sauce that is best made a day or two in advance, giving those citrusy cinnamon flavors a chance to really infuse.

INGREDIENTS

3 cups fresh or frozen cranberries
½ cup granulated sugar
1 cinnamon stick
¼ teaspoon freshly grated nutmeg
2 cloves
pared zest and juice
of 1 clementine

METHOD

1 Put all the ingredients in a small pan. Bring to a boil and simmer for 15 to 20 minutes, uncovered, stirring frequently, until the fruit begins to soften.

2 Gently crush some of the cranberries with the back of a spoon, leaving a few whole.

3 Set aside to cool completely, transfer to an airtight lidded container, and chill in the fridge overnight.

4 Before serving, remove the clementine zest strips, cinnamon stick, and cloves, and give the sauce a thorough stir.

SPICED
pumpkin butter

makes 1 × 12oz jar

If you are wondering what on earth pumpkin butter is, let me explain. I too had no idea what it was until I chanced upon some at a country store in the US and after the first mouthful I was hooked. Old school preserves, these so-called "butters" are far and beyond the fruit jams I'm used to in the UK, and this one is my favorite. I like to spread it on toast, dollop it in vegan yogurt, stir it through oatmeal, use it as a sweet dip with fruit, or, better still, eat it straight from the jar—I hope you love it as much as me!

INGREDIENTS

1 cup pumpkin purée (see step 1 of Pumpkin Pie recipe on page 151)
1/3 cup coconut or other plant milk
1/2 cup agave nectar or maple syrup
1/2 teaspoon cider vinegar
1 teaspoon vanilla extract
1 teaspoon ground cinnamon
1/2 teaspoon freshly grated nutmeg
1/4 teaspoon ground allspice
pinch of salt

METHOD

1 Place all the ingredients in a medium saucepan and bring to a gentle simmer, stirring frequently to prevent the mixture from sticking to the bottom of the pan. It should take approximately 20 to 30 minutes to thicken.

2 Preheat the oven to 300°F.

3 Sterilize a 12oz jar: wash it in very hot soapy water, rinse thoroughly, and dry in the oven for about 15 minutes. In the last 5 minutes, put the lid in the oven too.

4 When the butter has sufficiently thickened, transfer to the jar and screw the lid on immediately. Let it cool for at least a day before using or giving it away. Once opened, it will keep for 2 weeks in the fridge.

SWEET

Treats

CARROT CAKE BITES

CHOCOLATE PEANUT BUTTER BITES

CHOCOLATE BARK

FUDGY BROWNIES

CHOCOLATE CHESTNUT PIE

PUMPKIN PIE

SUGAR COOKIES THREE WAYS

MINT CHOCOLATE BIRTHDAY CAKE
WITH A GLOSSY GANACHE

SUMMER PUDDING

NECTARINE, BLUEBERRY, AND
ALMOND CRUMBLE

NO-BAKE STRAWBERRY
VANILLA CHEESECAKE

LEMON CURD

ALMOND CASHEW CREAM AND
COCOA CASHEW CREAM CUPS

BANANA, PEANUT BUTTER, AND
CHOCOLATE SAUCE SUNDAE

COINTREAU GRANITA

BAKED BANANAS IN A
CITRUS RUM SAUCE

AMARETTO BISCOTTI AND
EASY AFFOGATO

EASY CREAMY HORCHATA

carrot cake
BITES

Sweet treats don't necessarily have to be full of processed sugar. The natural sugars found in dates and raisins satisfy those cravings just as well as any chocolate bar or slice of fat-laden cake—but that's not to say you can't or shouldn't have the occasional piece. I'm increasingly conscious of how much cake I consume (welcome to your thirties!) and so I've taken inspiration from one of my all-time favorite recipes and given it a somewhat healthy twist by forming it into every seasoned vegan's standby sweet, the incomparable (but perhaps not so appetizingly named) "raw ball." And as an added bonus, these bite-sized treats don't even require any cooking—just process, roll, chill, and eat… now that's better than messing around with batter any day.

INGREDIENTS

1 small carrot, grated
1 cup medjool dates, pitted and roughly chopped
2¼ cups pecans
⅓ cup raisins
grated zest of 1 clementine or orange
¼ teaspoon ground cinnamon
¼ teaspoon ground ginger
pinch of freshly grated nutmeg
½ cup shredded coconut

METHOD

1 Squeeze out any excess liquid from the grated carrot.

2 Place all the ingredients, apart from the coconut, into a food processor and process until the mixture comes together in a large clump, scraping down the sides of the bowl a couple of times, if necessary.

3 Line a plate or baking sheet with parchment paper.

4 Take a teaspoon of the mixture, roll into a ball, and place on the parchment paper. Repeat to make 12 to 14 golfball-sized spheres in total.

5 Put the shredded coconut into a bowl and roll each ball in the coconut to coat. Place the balls on the lined plate and refrigerate overnight.

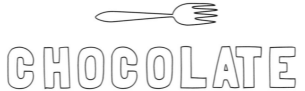

CHOCOLATE
peanut butter bites

makes 12

A "healthy treat" seems like a bit of an oxymoron—if it's healthy, it ain't a treat, right? However, these virtually guilt-free bites are just that, a sweet treat that smacks of sheer indulgence but without the refined sugar and fat normally associated with most desserts or confectionary. And should you want one, two, or more as a frequent afternoon snack, go right ahead. No problemo. The basic components you will need are soft nuts, such as walnuts or pecans, and some medjool dates, raisins, or golden raisins. The rest is up to you. Experiment with different flavors and combinations, use spices, extracts, whatever you think might work. Here, I've combined two of my own personal favorite ingredients—chocolate (cocoa) and peanut butter. For me, it doesn't get more indulgent or satisfying, because not only are you getting your chocolate fix, but those peanuts will give you a much-needed protein boost too.

INGREDIENTS

8 medjool dates, pitted,
or 1 cup raisins
½ cup pecans, chopped
2 tablespoons crunchy
peanut butter
1 tablespoon cocoa powder, plus
extra for dusting
1 tablespoon date syrup

METHOD

1 Line a plate or baking sheet with parchment paper.

2 Put all the ingredients in a food processor and process until the mixture resembles coarse bread crumbs.

3 Transfer the mixture into a bowl and roll it into 12 equal-sized balls. Place on the lined pan or plate and chill in the fridge overnight.

4 To serve, place a little sifted cocoa powder on a plate and carefully roll each ball until coated. Shake off any excess cocoa powder before serving.

chocolate BARK

serves 2 to 4

Sometimes the simpler the sweet, the better, and it really doesn't get much simpler than this decadent Chocolate Bark—so called because of its bark-like appearance when broken into shards. Basically, this is just an exercise in melting, but you can have fun choosing the toppings… with results that belie the recipe's easy reality (shhh, I won't tell if you won't!). Wrap it in pretty tissue paper and pop it in a vintage tin and you have one impressive gift that has that desirable homemade vibe—*et voilà!*

INGREDIENTS

7oz good-quality dark chocolate
(minimum 70 percent cocoa
solids), broken into pieces
pinch of sea salt

Topping choices
coarse sea salt
cacao nibs
crushed candy canes
chopped nuts

METHOD

1 Line a shallow 8in baking sheet with parchment paper.

2 Bring a small pan of water to a boil and then turn down to barely a simmer. Put a heatproof bowl on top, add the chocolate and salt, and melt, stirring every so often.

3 When the chocolate has melted, pour into the lined baking sheet and spread out using a spatula—the shape is irrelevant; just make sure you don't spread it too thinly. Sprinkle with your chosen toppings. Let cool and set at room temperature and then, once it is solid, break it into pieces.

fudgy BROWNIES

makes 12 to 16

You'd be hard pressed to find somebody who doesn't love a good brownie. While everyone has their very personal views on how gooey or chewy brownies should be, my favored texture errs on the fudgy side. Chunky enough to cut into manageable bite-sized squares, these could also eat be eaten warm with a scoop of dairy-free vanilla ice cream for a truly indulgent dessert. Enjoy!

INGREDIENTS

2 cups all-purpose flour
1 teaspoon baking powder
pinch of salt
1 banana, peeled and mashed
1¼ cups superfine sugar
1 tablespoon vanilla extract
5½oz good-quality dark chocolate (minimum 70 percent cocoa solids), broken into pieces
4 tablespoons vegan margarine, plus extra for greasing
1 tablespoon agave nectar
⅓ cup dark chocolate chips
1 cup walnuts, chopped
confectioners' sugar, to dust

METHOD

1 Preheat the oven to 350°F. Grease an 8in baking pan and line with parchment paper.

2 Sift the flour, baking powder, and salt into a large bowl.

3 In a medium bowl, combine the mashed banana, sugar, and vanilla extract.

4 Bring a small pan of water to a boil and then turn down to barely a simmer. Put a heatproof bowl on top, place the chocolate, margarine, and agave in the bowl, and melt together until smooth and glossy. Pour the melted chocolate into the banana mix and stir to combine.

5 Make a well in the center of the flour, pour in the chocolate mixture, and fold thoroughly until everything is incorporated. Finally, fold in the chocolate chips and walnuts, ensuring not to overwork the batter.

6 Pour into the prepared pan and bake in the oven for 25 minutes.

7 Let cool completely before cutting into pieces and dusting the brownies with confectioners' sugar.

chocolate chestnut
PIE

serves 8 to 12

Indulgence is definitely not off-limits when it comes to vegan desserts. This wonderfully rich pie is seriously decadent and makes use of an ingredient normally reserved for Christmas… the humble chestnut. Supermarkets generally stock chestnut products year-round, so you can whip up this impressive pie on a whim.

INGREDIENTS

For the sweetened coconut cream
1 cup UHT coconut cream, chilled overnight
3 tablespoons agave nectar
1 teaspoon vanilla extract

For the crust
2½ cups dairy-free graham crackers, crushed into crumbs
1 heaping tablespoon cocoa powder
2 tablespoons agave nectar
3 tablespoons soy butter

For the topping
1 × 14oz can sweetened chestnut purée
3½oz good-quality dark chocolate (minimum 70 percent cocoa solids), broken into pieces
2 tablespoons agave nectar
1 teaspoon vanilla extract
9oz sweetened chestnut spread
grated chocolate, to decorate

METHOD

1 Line the bottom of a 4½in-deep, 8in round cake pan with parchment paper.

2 Put the chilled coconut cream a in bowl, add the agave nectar and vanilla extract, and whisk until thick. Keep in fridge until required.

3 For the crust, place the graham cracker crumbs in a large bowl. Add the cocoa powder and agave. Melt the soy butter in a small pan, pour it over the graham cracker crumbs, and stir to combine. Cover the bottom of the lined pan with the crumb mixture and press it firmly using the back of a spoon until compacted. Refrigerate for at least 20 minutes or until firm.

4 For the topping, place the purée into a large bowl. Bring a small pan of water to a boil and then turn down to barely a simmer. Put a heatproof bowl on top, add the chocolate, and melt, stirring every so often. Stir the melted chocolate into the purée, followed by the agave nectar and vanilla extract, ensuring everything is thoroughly combined.

5 Pour half the purée mixture onto the crumb crust and use a spatula to spread it evenly to the edges of the pan. Place in the fridge for at least 1 hour before spreading over the chestnut spread. Return to the fridge for another 20 to 30 minutes or until the spread has set. Top with the remaining chestnut purée mixture. Refrigerate for at least 1 hour or preferably overnight.

6 Sprinkle with grated chocolate and serve with the coconut cream.

PUMPKIN
pie

serves 5 to 8

While this dessert is a Thanksgiving staple in the US, it's not exactly commonplace elsewhere…
more fool us, I cry! Not only can I claim to be a fully-fledged member of the pumpkin-pie club, thanks
to an educational and delicious stint in Chicago, but I'm also determined to spread the good word wherever
I go. My first Thanksgiving remains one of my fondest memories of our time in Chi-town, so we've now
adopted this holiday as our own and celebrate it every year, even down in the depths of Cornwall. This
dish is living (or should that be eating?) proof that you don't need to be American to be Thankful, nor
do you have to like pumpkin to be able to enjoy this pie.

INGREDIENTS

1 pumpkin, halved and seeds
scooped out
5½oz firm silken tofu
1 teaspoon ground cinnamon
½ teaspoon ground allspice
¼ teaspoon freshly grated nutmeg
½ cup dark brown sugar
½ cup agave nectar
3 tablespoons maple syrup
1 teaspoon cornstarch
soy cream or non-dairy ice cream,
to serve

For the crust
7oz gingersnap cookies
(about 28 cookies)
2 tablespoons vegan butter

METHOD

1 Preheat the oven to 400°F. Place the pumpkin halves flesh-side down in a large baking dish. Pour in 1 cup water and roast until completely soft, about 60 minutes. Let cool before scooping out the flesh with a spoon and puréeing in a blender. This will yield about 2 cups purée—you won't need it all. Reduce oven temperature to 350°F.

2 For the crust, process or smash the cookies into crumbs and transfer to a bowl. Melt the vegan butter in a small pan, pour it over the crumbs, and stir to combine. Cover the bottom of an 8in pie dish with the crumb mixture and press it firmly using the back of a spoon until compacted and rising slightly up the sides of the dish. Refrigerate for at least 10 minutes.

3 Blend 1 cup of the pumpkin puree with the remaining ingredients in a food processor until smooth, then pour into the chilled crust. Place the pie on a baking sheet and bake in the oven for 40 minutes or until just set (it should still have some wobble). Turn the oven off and leave the pie in the oven for another 20 minutes.

4 Remove the pie from the oven and let it cool before serving (or refrigerate overnight). Serve the pie at room temperature or chilled, with soy cream or non-dairy ice cream.

sugar COOKIES

makes 6 large cookies

This basic cookie recipe is very well tried and trusted—great for when you want something to go with a cup of coffee or you just like having a fail-safe play in the kitchen. I don't like making huge batches of cookies because, quite frankly, I will just sit down and eat them in one fell swoop—call it portion control or a distinct lack of will power, but small batches always work for me. Of course, if you have guests or are baking for a crowd, simply double, triple, or quadruple the quantities to suit. Just don't skip the refrigeration step or your cookies will fall more than a little flat. Once chilled, the dough keeps in the fridge for up to 1 week, so you can have freshly baked cookies in around 20 minutes. And check out the variations, too—there's something for everyone… personally, I like the stuffed sandwiches the best but maybe that's because I'm greedy. Enjoy!

INGREDIENTS

9 tablespoons vegan butter
2/3 cup granulated sugar
1 teaspoon vanilla extract
2 cup all-purpose flour
1 teaspoon baking powder

METHOD

1 Cream the butter and sugar in a large bowl until fluffy. Stir in the vanilla extract and mix thoroughly.

2 In a separate bowl combine the flour and baking powder. Add the flour to the creamed butter and mix until a soft dough is formed.

3 Shape into a log, wrap in plastic wrap or foil, and refrigerate for at least an hour or preferably overnight.

4 To bake, preheat the oven to 350°F. Divide and roll the cookie dough into 6 equal-sized balls before spacing them well apart on a baking sheet.

5 Bake in batches, allowing 15 to 20 minutes for each batch—a little underdone is best as the cookies will firm up when cooled.

6 Let cool on the baking sheet for a few minutes, then carefully transfer them to a wire cooling rack.

FOR LEMON DRIZZLE COOKIES

Make the cookies as opposite, adding the zest and juice of 1 lemon to the creamed mixture. Add up to 3 tablespoons extra flour to the dough if needed. Let cool for at least an hour before icing. Mix ¾ cup confectioners' sugar with 3 to 5 teaspoons lemon juice to form a smooth icing. Drizzle over the cookies and sprinkle with lemon zest. Allow to set before serving.

FOR DOUBLE CHOCOLATE CHIP COOKIES

Make the cookies as opposite, adding 1 tablespoon cocoa powder and ½ cup chocolate chips to the flour mixture.

FOR STUFFED COOKIE SANDWICHES

Make one batch of basic cookies as opposite and set aside to cool. Whisk together 7 tablespoons vegan butter, ½ cup confectioners' sugar, and 1 teaspoon vanilla extract until fluffy. Sandwich a generous layer of the buttercream between two cookies just before serving. Enjoy!

MINT CHOCOLATE
BIRTHDAY CAKE
with a glossy ganache
serves 8 to 10

I'm going all out with this one… well, it is a birthday cake after all. Chocolate-clad and with a minty buttercream filling, it was actually the result of a rather unfortunate incident that basically amounted to me entirely forgetting my husband's birthday (eek!). In my panic, I cobbled together whatever I had in the cupboards and fridge and—bingo!—this b-day cake was born, and a minor crisis averted in the process, phew. Moist, sweet, minty—this has since become my go-to chocolate cake recipe.

INGREDIENTS

For the cake
1 1/3 cups all-purpose flour
1/2 cup cocoa powder
1 cup superfine sugar
1 teaspoon baking powder
1/2 teaspoon baking soda
1/2 teaspoon salt
1 cup warm water
1/3 cup sunflower oil
1 teaspoon vanilla extract
1 teaspoon cider vinegar

*For the peppermint
buttercream filling*
1 tablespoon vegan butter
1 cup unrefined
confectioners' sugar
2 teaspoons good-quality
peppermint extract
1 tablespoon soy milk

METHOD

1 Preheat the oven to 350°F. Line the bottom and sides of a 4in-deep, 8in round cake pan with parchment paper.

2 In a large bowl, combine the flour, cocoa powder, sugar, baking powder, baking soda, and salt. Mix thoroughly. In a separate bowl, whisk together the water, oil, vanilla extract, and cider vinegar.

3 Make a well in the center of the flour mixture and pour in the wet ingredients, lightly folding until a smooth, fairly runny batter forms.

4 Transfer the cake mixture to the prepared pan and bake for 40 to 50 minutes. The cake is ready when a skewer inserted into the center comes out clean.

6 Remove the cake from the oven and let it cool completely in the pan before transferring it to a wire cooling rack. Carefully halve the cold cake horizontally, using a sharp knife.

7 For the buttercream, combine all the ingredients in a bowl and beat together until completely smooth, adding a little more soy milk if necessary.

8 Spread the buttercream mixture on the bottom cake layer and carefully place the other half on top.

INGREDIENTS

For the dark chocolate ganache
¼ cup soy milk
1 teaspoon vegan butter
5½oz good-quality dark
chocolate, (minimum 70 percent
cocoa solids), broken into pieces

METHOD

⑨ For the ganache, place the soy milk and butter in a small, heavy-bottomed pan and gently heat until the butter melts. Add the chocolate pieces and stir until you achieve a smooth, glossy mixture.

⑩ Let cool for several minutes before carefully pouring over the cake. Spread the ganache over the whole cake using a palette knife. Put the cake aside until the ganache is cool—it will set slightly. Once it is set, cut the cake into slices to serve. It will keep in a cake pan, covered, for several days.

SUMMER
pudding

serves 4

Puddings are not high on my priority eat list in the middle of a hot summer, but I'll make an exception for this one. It's light and fresh (and thankfully can be prepared in advance), making it the perfect choice for an easy lunch. The mint and lemon lend an added dimension to the flavor, but whatever you do, make sure your bread is top notch quality otherwise it will really impair the taste.

INGREDIENTS

1¼lb fresh or frozen mixed berries
1 cup granulated sugar
grated zest and juice of 1 lemon
sprig of mint, plus extra leaves,
to decorate
10 slices white bread (about
½in thick) crusts removed

METHOD

1 Place the berries in a pan along with the sugar, lemon juice, and mint sprig. Bring to a boil and then reduce to a gentle simmer for several minutes until the berries begin to exude their juices and soften. Make sure they don't soften too much. Remove from the heat and let cool completely before removing the mint sprig and stirring through the lemon zest.

2 Cut all but 4 slices of the bread into triangles.

3 Dip the bread triangles in the fruit mixture so they soak up the juices. Use the bread to line 4 tea cups or deep ramekins, ensuring there are no gaps, and then fill each with one-quarter of the fruit. Cut 4 circles from the remaining bread to fit on top of the fruit. Put in place and press firmly so the bread soaks up some of the juices.

4 Spoon any remaining juices over the puddings. Refrigerate overnight with weights on top.

5 To serve, loosen each pudding gently with a knife and place a small serving plate on top of the cup. Holding the cup securely in place, invert the plate. Gently tap the cup with the handle of a knife until the pudding slips out.

6 Decorate with mint leaves and serve with dairy-free cream.

NECTARINE, BLUEBERRY, and almond CRUMBLE

serves 4 to 6

I have a tendency to shy away from refined sugar because I feel the taste can often be replicated just as well with vegan sweeteners such as agave nectar or maple syrup. In this case, however, I can emphatically say it's sugar all the way. Nothing beats a good crumble and, having practically grown up on it, I think I know a thing or two about this staple dessert. The combination of the tart nectarines with the almondy topping is a thing of sheer beauty, and even though I usually spin a semi-cautionary tale of sugar consumption in extreme moderation, when it comes to this dessert I encourage you to throw caution entirely to the wind and relish in its über comforting (sugar-filled) joy.

INGREDIENTS

vegan margarine, for greasing
4 nectarines, halved and pitted
1 cup blueberries
3 tablespoons sugar
1 teaspoon vanilla extract
dairy-free custard, ice cream, or cream, to serve

For the crumble
1 cup all-purpose flour
¾ cup almond flour
pinch of salt
½ teaspoon baking powder
3 tablespoons vegan margarine
½ cup sliced almonds, toasted
2 tablespoons sugar

METHOD

1 Preheat the oven to 350°F. Lightly grease a baking dish, approximately 8 × 12in.

2 Place the nectarines, cut side down, in the dish. Evenly sprinkle the blueberries and sugar over the nectarines and drizzle with the vanilla extract.

3 In a medium mixing bowl, combine the flour, almond flour, salt, and baking powder. Add the margarine and lightly rub into the flour mixture with your fingertips until the mixture resembles fine bread crumbs. Gently stir in the sliced almonds and half the sugar. Disperse the crumble evenly over the fruit before topping with a final dusting of sugar.

4 Bake in the oven for 25 to 30 minutes until the fruit begins to bubble over the crumble and the sugary top has become golden.

5 Let cool for a few minutes before serving with dairy-free custard, ice cream, or cream—or all three!

NO-BAKE
strawberry vanilla cheesecake
serves 8 to 10

Rich, decadent, and the antithesis of how vegan sweets are normally perceived, this no-bake cheeseless cheesecake will fool everyone and, who knows, may even convert the most fervent of dairy fans. Strictly speaking, authentically raw cheesecakes do not use processed sweeteners such as agave nectar, but seeing as I'm not inclined to be too dogmatic about things, I think we can be a little flexible—especially when it tastes this good! This is a real showstopper of a dessert and no one will be able to guess what the main ingredient is. You'll need to start making it well in advance as the stars of the show need soaking for at least 6 hours.

INGREDIENTS

For the crust
2 cups pecans
½ cup medjool dates, pitted

For the strawberry layer
1¼ cups strawberries, hulled
2 tablespoons lemon juice
3 tablespoons agave nectar or maple syrup
1 cup cashews, soaked in cold water for 6 hours and drained

For the vanilla layer
2½ cups cashews, soaked in cold water for 6 hours and drained
½ cup agave nectar
seeds from 1 vanilla bean
juice of ½ lemon
¼ cup filtered water

METHOD

1 Place the crust ingredients in a food processor or blender and blend until crumbly. Line an 8in loose-bottomed cake pan with parchment paper and turn the crust mixture into it. Press the mixture firmly to the edges of the pan using the back of your fingers or a spoon. Place in the freezer for 30 minutes.

2 Process the strawberries for the strawberry layer together with 1 tablespoon of the lemon juice and 1 tablespoon of the agave, then strain through a sieve.

3 Blend the drained cashews for the strawberry layer with the strawberry sauce and the remainder of the lemon juice and agave until completely smooth, scraping down the sides periodically. Taste for sweetness; if you prefer it sweeter, add a little more agave. If you are using maple syrup instead, be careful not to add too much as it will make it really runny.

4 Remove the crust from the freezer and carefully pour in the strawberry cheesecake mixture. Smooth with a spatula until it is completely even and return to the freezer for 1 hour.

5 Meanwhile, place all the ingredients for the vanilla layer in the blender and process until completely smooth. This layer will be less thick and almost more like a cashew cream. When the strawberry layer has set, carefully pour

INGREDIENTS

For the marinated strawberries
½ cup strawberries,
hulled and sliced
1 teaspoon vanilla extract

METHOD

in the vanilla mixture. Smooth with a spatula and return to the freezer for several hours.

6 Place the sliced strawberries in a bowl along with the vanilla extract to marinate for at least 1 hour.

7 When the cheesecake has set, transfer to the fridge for 30 minutes before removing it from the pan. Serve with the marinated strawberries.

lemon
CURD

makes 1 × 16oz jar

I have a very strong memory of making myself lemon curd sandwiches as a child—it actually may have been the first thing I ever made in the kitchen. Of course, traditional curd is made with egg, but I was determined to find a way of replicating it *sans* animal products when I became vegan. Possessing no obvious trace of its coconut milk base, this sweet and tangy spread is just heavenly on anything from toast to croissants and even vegan scones… childhood memory safely intact.

INGREDIENTS

4 lemons
1 × 14oz can coconut milk
½ cup superfine sugar
2 to 3 tablespoons cornstarch

METHOD

1 Finely grate the zest of 1 of the lemons and remove the zest of another in wide strips using a vegetable peeler. Squeeze the juice from all 4 of the lemons.

2 Place the lemon juice, zest, and zest strips in a small, heavy-bottomed saucepan with the coconut milk, superfine sugar, and cornstarch (for a runnier consistency use 2 tablespoons of cornstarch but for a denser, more spreadable curd, add 3) and whisk together until thoroughly combined.

3 Bring to a boil and then simmer uncovered for about 1 hour, stirring frequently, until the mixture reduces and thickens.

4 Preheat the oven to 325°F.

5 Sterilize a 16oz lidded glass jar by running it through the dishwasher or by washing it in very hot soapy water, rinsing thoroughly, and drying in the oven for about 15 minutes. In the last 5 minutes, put the lid in the oven too.

6 Set the lemon curd aside to cool before discarding the strips of zest. Transfer the curd to the sterilized jar. Seal and store. Once opened, this will keep in the fridge for 2 weeks.

ALMOND CASHEW CREAM
and cocoa cashew
CREAM CUPS

serves 2 to 4

Cashews are endlessly versatile and, even though you begin with the same basic cream, these two dairy-free cream desserts couldn't taste more different. It's worthwhile keeping a batch of both in your fridge at all times—y'know, in case of any last-minute dessert emergencies. Well, that's my excuse anyway.

ALMOND CASHEW CREAM

2 cups cashews, soaked in water
for at least 6 hours
1 teaspoon almond extract
3 tablespoons agave nectar
pinch of salt
peeled fresh peaches and sliced
almonds, to serve

1 Place the cashews in a blender with ⅔ cup water. Process until smooth (they will go through several stages... nutty, grainy, coarse, and smooth), adding a little extra water if necessary and scraping down the sides as you go. Add the almond extract, agave, and salt. Process until completely smooth. Refrigerate for at least an hour.

2 Pour the cashew cream over the peaches and decorate with sliced almonds.

COCOA CASHEW CREAM CUPS

For the cream
As above, but replace the almond
extract with 1 tablespoon rose
orange blossom water and
1 heaping tablespoon cocoa
powder

For the crust
¾ cup unsalted pistachio nuts
4 medjool dates, pitted
fresh raspberries and crushed
pistachios, to serve

1 Prepare the cream as in step 1 above, but reduce the water to ⅓ cup and add the cocoa powder and rose or orange blossom water instead of the almond extract. The consistency will be thicker for this cream.

2 For the crust, place the pistachios and dates in a food processor and process until they resemble coarse bread crumbs. Press into four individual tart rounds or silicone cupcake liners and place in the freezer for at least 1 hour.

3 Carefully remove the crust shells from the rounds or liners and spoon in the cocoa cashew mixture. Top with fresh raspberries and crushed pistachios.

BANANA, PEANUT BUTTER,
and chocolate sauce
SUNDAE

serves 2

Who says ice cream has to be unhealthy? This banana-based sundae is every bit as satisfying as its dairy-clad counterpart but with a quarter of the guilt. The saltiness of the peanut butter is perfectly offset by the sweetness of the chocolate, and makes for one heck of a finish to any meal or even to be enjoyed on its own as a special stand-alone treat. I will hold my hand up at this point and admit to having a bit of a thing for peanut butter (and indeed bananas… and maybe even dark chocolate too), so it's not exactly a shocker that I'd want to combine all three in one lavishly tall sundae glass and eat unashamedly with the requisite über long spoon until I feel slightly sick but certainly satisfied—I am, after all, human, and, more significantly, a girl.

INGREDIENTS

4 bananas
2 tablespoons maple syrup or other vegan sweetener
1 heaping teaspoon smooth peanut butter

For the sauce
¼ cup soy milk
3½oz good-quality dark chocolate (minimum 70 percent cocoa solids), broken into small pieces
1 tablespoon agave nectar
handful of roughly chopped salted peanuts, to serve

METHOD

1 Peel the bananas and chop into large chunks. Place in an airtight lidded container, secure the lid, and freeze overnight.

2 Place the frozen banana pieces in a bowl and process with a hand-held blender until smooth and creamy—this will take a few minutes. Scrape down the sides with a spatula now and then.

3 Add the maple syrup and peanut butter to the blended bananas and process together. Place this ice cream mixture in the lidded container and pop in the freezer while you make the sauce.

4 Place the soy milk, dark chocolate, and agave nectar in a heavy-bottomed saucepan and melt over low heat, gently stirring with a spatula to incorporate. It may look grainy initially, but will eventually become smooth and glossy.

5 Spoon the ice cream into tall glasses and pour the hot sauce over the top, topping it all off with a sprinkling of salted peanuts.

cointreau GRANITA

serves 4 to 6

Almost like an ice-slushy for grown-ups, this Cointreau-infused granita is a wonderful palate cleanser as well as being a nice alternative to the more commonly served sorbet. It takes a little attention to get it just the right consistency but the refreshing results are definitely worth it—especially if you're a Cointreau fan like me. It might be a bad habit of mine, but I frequently find myself thinking of ways to inject alcohol into food— sweet, savory, both are up for grabs. In this case, the alcohol also acts as an ice crystal deterrent, meaning the granita will never become too solid and will keep well in the freezer until you need it.

INGREDIENTS

grated zest and juice of
2 large oranges
grated zest and juice of 1 lime
½ cup superfine sugar
1 teaspoon orange extract
3 to 4 tablespoons Cointreau,
plus extra to serve
dark chocolate squares, to serve

METHOD

1 Place 1 cup water, the orange and lime zest and juice, sugar, and orange extract in a small pan. Bring to a steady boil for around a minute or until the sugar has completely dissolved.

2 Let cool slightly before adding the Cointreau. Transfer to a lidded airtight container and freeze. After an hour or so, scrape the frozen granita until it becomes slush-like, and repeat every 30 minutes for several hours until you achieve the desired consistency.

3 Spoon into glass serving dishes, drizzle with an additional splash of Cointreau, and top with squares of dark chocolate.

BAKED BANANAS
in a citrus
RUM SAUCE

serves 2 to 3

I don't know about you, but I eat a lot of bananas. Not exactly indigenous to where I live, they come laden with a carbon footprint, I will concede, that would make most environmentalists weep. But us vegans need our vices too, y'know, so the bananas stay. In such situations where your conscience is getting the better of you, I find a dash of rum always helps. Sugar is also a soother. Combine the two and you're onto a surefire winner. Even if you have issues with baked fruit, I would gently suggest you try these sweet and sticky sliced bananas before making your final decision on the matter. They are great served cold but I love them warm with a generous topping of vegan whipped cream—if we're being naughty, we might as well go for it...

INGREDIENTS

3 large ripe bananas
2 tablespoons brown sugar
¼ teaspoon freshly grated nutmeg
½ teaspoon ground cinnamon
2 to 3 star anise (optional)
¼ cup rum
juice of 1 clementine or orange
juice of ½ lime
2 tablespoons date syrup
vegan whipped cream and freshly
grated nutmeg, to serve

METHOD

1 Preheat the oven to 350°F.

2 Peel the bananas and halve them lengthwise. Place them in an heatproof dish and sprinkle with the sugar, nutmeg, cinnamon, and star anise (if using). Lightly toss so they are coated all over, then bake for 10 minutes.

3 Meanwhile, whisk together the rum, clementine juice, lime juice, and date syrup. Pour over the bananas and bake for another 15 to 20 minutes. Remove from the oven when the sauce is bubbling and the bananas have browned.

4 Allow the bananas to cool for 10 minutes—they will still be warm. Alternatively, let them cool completely and refrigerate.

5 Serve warm or cold with a generous helping of whipped cream and a dusting of freshly grated nutmeg. The perfect summer treat.

amaretto biscotti and easy
AFFOGATO

serves 4

When I first became vegan, the baking side of things really flummoxed me. I had no idea what to use in place of eggs and it really felt as if I were learning to cook all over again. Applesauce turned out to be an absolute life-saver. This simple biscotti recipe always gets an "ooh" reaction when I present it at dinner parties… coupled with the affogato, it truly is an impressive finish to any meal.

INGREDIENTS

For the biscotti
1 cup all-purpose flour, plus extra for dusting
²/₃ cup almond flour
¹/₄ teaspoon baking powder
¹/₄ teaspoon baking soda
pinch of salt
3 tablespoons applesauce
3 tablespoons olive oil
3 tablespoons Amaretto
¹/₄ cup superfine sugar
¹/₃ cup hazelnuts, chopped

For the affogato
¹/₄ cup espresso or strong ground coffee
2 tablespoons Amaretto
4 scoops good-quality vegan ice cream

METHOD

1 Preheat the oven to 350°F. Grease a 9in baking sheet and line with parchment paper.

2 In a large bowl, sift the flour, almond flour, baking powder, baking soda, and salt together. In another bowl, whisk the applesauce, oil, Amaretto, and sugar together until thoroughly combined.

3 Make a well in the center of the flour mix and pour in the wet ingredients. Fold gently with a spatula until the mixture comes together, but don't overwork it. Lightly stir in the hazelnuts and, using your hands, form it into a soft dough before turning it onto a floured surface.

4 Shape the mixture into a log about ¹/₂in thick and score the top with a knife—this will make it easier to cut into bars later. Transfer to the prepared baking sheet and bake for 30 minutes. Remove from the oven and turn the temperature down to 300°F. Let the log cool slightly before cutting it into 8 to 10 bars. Set aside until completely cool.

5 Return to the oven for 10 minutes. Turn each biscotto over and bake for a final 10 minutes. Transfer to a wire rack and let cool completely.

6 Place the coffee in a french press and pour in ³/₄ cup freshly boiled water. Steep for 5 minutes, then add the Amaretto and press the plunger. Scoop the ice cream into coffee cups, pour over the coffee, and serve with the biscotti.

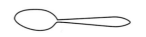

easy creamy HORCHATA

serves 2

I was first introduced to this traditional Mexican drink in Chicago. Luckily for us we lived in a district teeming with wondrous Mexican food outlets and I quickly became obsessed with this refreshingly creamy beverage that is actually naturally vegan—yay! It's usually made with rice, but I find this oat alternative to be equally yummy—the bonus being that it takes a fraction of the time to prepare. I often make it during the summer and chill it in the fridge prior to serving. Double, triple, or quadruple the quantities and serve it in crowd-pleasing caraffes… plus, you could even throw in a splash of rum for parties. Now, who could say no to that?!

METHOD

2¾ cups rolled oats
1 small cinnamon stick
¼ cup maple syrup or
agave nectar
ice cubes, to serve

1 Blend the oats with 2 cups water and the cinnamon stick until smooth. Add the sweetener and blend again.

2 Strain through a fine-mesh sieve or cheesecloth and serve over lots of ice.

Variations

Try adding 1 tablespoon cocoa powder, 1 tablespoon vanilla extract, or a dash of freshly grated nutmeg for an extra twist.

INDEX

ACKNOWLEDGMENTS

A thousand thanks to Kyle Books for giving me the opportunity to fulfill my lifelong dream of writing a cookbook. A special thanks to Judith for thinking I had something to say, and also to my wonderful Editor Tara, for all her patience, guidance, and unflinching calm demeanor. It's been a truly incredible experience for which I will always be grateful.

Thanks also to Ali Allen for her magical photography skills, Linda Tubby for her styling genius, and Nicky Collings for her magnificent design, which have all brought the book to life in the best possible way. Thanks also to Abbi-Rose for the incredible make-up and hair, and Nicola at Beautiful Soul for the heavenly wardrobe.

To the many friends who have helped me along the way, I also owe a debt of gratitude, especially Nathan, Brendan, and Rebecca—thank you, thank you, thank you!

Thanks to my mentor David Hayes for giving me the confidence to believe in myself when I most needed it.

As ever, an enormous amount of thanks goes to my entire family back in Derry—you will never know how much you have brightened my life.

To my pal (Joey) Joanne Doherty, for her loyalty and friendship. To my Nanny and Granda for just always being so lovely to me—I adore you. To my wonderful, talented, sister, Mairead, for being the best friend a girl could ask for. To my parents Hugo and Marie, for their unending love and support—you are everything to me.

Finally, one colossal thank you to the love of my life, my beautiful Jason, who completes my life and makes me laugh every day.